Millennial Marxist

MATTHEW JOHN

For Hannah

Copyright © 2022 Matthew John
All rights reserved

Published by Matthew John

ISBN 978-1-257-83000-8

Contents

Preface ... 7

Part I

Under Capitalism, a Pandemic Is a Time of Political Awakening ... 15

White Supremacy and Capitalism: The Two-Headed Dragon that Must Be Slain ... 18

5 Commonly Whitewashed Aspects of Dr. King's Life and Death ... 23

6 Disturbing Aspects of American Policing ... 31

It's Time To Abolish Columbus Day ... 37

The 2001 Terrorist Attack on American Soil Wasn't the Only '9/11' ... 41

Part II

Does the U.S. Government Really Care about Syrian Civilians? ... 47

White Nationalist Terror and Anti-Fascist Resistance ... 50

New Prospects for the Left Amid Extreme Wealth Concentration ... 55

Bipartisan Brutality Toward the People of El Salvador ... 58

On Russiagate ... 61

Trump's Muslim Ban Has Nothing to Do With National Security ... 65

It's Time for Progressives to Boycott Israel ... 68

The 'Resistance' Cheers for Assange's Arrest ... 73

The Ballot and the Bullet: Building Socialism in 'America's Backyard' ... 76

A Journalist Was Arrested and the Mainstream Media Was Silent ... 82

Impeachment is a Ruling-Class Spectacle ... 85

Why I'm Voting for Bernie Sanders ... 87

Lessons in Confronting America's Anti-Cuba Political Dogma ... 92

Why I Won't Vote for Biden or Trump ... 94

Imperialist Propaganda and the New Cold War With China ... 101

Why Liberals Can't Shame Progressives into Voting for Biden ... 105

Coronavirus and American Exceptionalism ... 108

Remembering Guaidó's Last Stand ... 111

The Unavoidable Irony of Mike Pompeo's Holocaust Statement ... 115

Professional Oppression and Identity Politics ... 117

Ruth Bader Ginsburg and the Limits of Liberal Feminism ... 120

Fear and Loathing on Election Day 2020 ... 128

While Heartening, The Chauvin Verdict Is Still an Outlier ... 131

Part III *(or "Lessons for the Left")*

Acknowledgements ... 145

Online Presence ... 147

Notes ... 148

Preface

The book you are currently holding in your hands (or gazing at through the glowing screen of your preferred electronic device) provides an introduction to the leftist and progressive political views that have recently become more prevalent in the United States. If you're wondering who I am or what gave me the nerve to write a book, let me briefly explain my credentials and my origin story (excluding the graphic details of my birth).

Let's start in 2007, when I graduated from college with a Bachelor of Fine Arts degree in photography. After first serving in AmeriCorps for one year, I began looking for a job in my field of study amid a frenetic financial crisis and the subsequent Great Recession. The job search proved rather difficult and frustrating. Every place I applied to either wasn't hiring or was actively downsizing. This went on for months. I couldn't help but partially blame myself, although I later found out that more than eight million Americans[1] lost their jobs in this economic nightmare. I guess I was in the wrong place at the wrong time.

Eventually, I settled for a series of restaurant and manual labor jobs, still applying to countless "better" jobs in my spare time. My inability to find a job in my field was disheartening in its own right, but I also had to worry about paying my exorbitant monthly student loan payments. Despite a few freelance gigs over the years, I never found a full-time job in my field of study, and, due to predatory interest rates, my total student loan debt is still about the same as it was when I graduated—around $100,000. Although I have been consistently working full-time for about a decade and a half (sometimes two jobs), I have yet to attain financial stability.

My story is by no means unique. In fact, almost 80 percent[2] of American workers live paycheck-to-paycheck, 44 percent of Americans[3] can't afford a $400 emergency, and 45 million Americans[4] are burdened with a cumulative $1.7 trillion in student loan debt. As I have personally discovered, these precarious material conditions can often till the soil for political radicalization. The question is whether one will be pushed to the left or to the right.

* * *

Writing is probably the one thing in my life that has remained constant. It runs in my family, so it's practically involuntary. I have kept journals as long as I can remember, and in college I began writing outlandish stories—both fiction and non-fiction—for the school newspaper. I also wrote a polemic called something like, "Jesus Christ vs. George W. Bush." Thinking back, that may have been my first official written work of political commentary. History and liberal studies professors seemed to give me more positive feedback on my writing than professors in my own field of study. Maybe I should have taken the hint.

Back then I was an anarcho-curious liberal, having previously read Howard Zinn, Noam Chomsky, and Michael Moore books during my bookstore gig fresh out of high school. I was vehemently anti-Bush, often incorporating him and his fiendish posse into my visual art projects. I attended many local Iraq War protests, taking photos and chanting with the crowds. I casually chatted with cops who were present, not yet knowing they are our class enemies.

Around that time, I interned at an organization called Peace Action —a small, seemingly anti-imperialist outfit staffed by long-haired white folks who raised awareness of the horrors of U.S. foreign policy. Bush was conducting mass murder against innocent civilians and I knew he needed to be stopped. I decided to canvass door-to-door for Kerry/Edwards 2004 in my spare time. The Johns. Sure, both parties sucked, but this was really about defeating Bush – the most dangerous president in our lifetimes.

Fast-forward to 2016. Despite espousing what I vaguely referred to as "socialist" views for many years, the election of Donald Trump immediately awakened a dormant radicalism in me. I soon found myself participating in a counter-protest that was confronting a "White Lives Matter" rally, complete with masked antifa warriors, riot police, and armed Maoists. This harsh new hyper-American reality began broadening my political horizons. I knew what I was witnessing around me wasn't acceptable, but I didn't quite know the correct analysis or the path forward.

A lot was happening and I wanted to make sense of it. Dusting off my most trusty skill, I decided to start writing political commentary. Hell, I had already been doing so for years in the form of vitriolic social media arguments anyway. As I read more and wrote more, my views became more refined. I thought more about the systemic failures of progressive activism, the tangible barriers to working-class solidarity, and the important historical and internationalist analyses that were omitted from leftist discourse. My recent political journey is apparent in these pages and is surely relatable to others.

What I have assembled in this volume is a series of essays, op-eds, and polemics written during the four-year period between April 2017 and April 2021. A handful of the pieces featured here were also published by a working-class think tank called the Hampton Institute (named after the famous Black Panther Fred Hampton). This organization was founded "with the purpose of giving a platform to everyday, working-class people to theorize, comment, analyze, and discuss matters that exist outside the confines of their daily lives, yet greatly impact them on a daily basis."[5] The proletarian framework of the Hampton Institute stuck with me, providing more confidence to continue writing political commentary without feeling as though I lacked the proper credentials.

I am and always have been a working-class Joe. My first job was a paper route at around age 13. I then worked at a local pizza joint on the weekends for most of high school. My subsequent jobs included forklift driver, warehouse worker, server, coffee roaster, "event operations staff," circuit board assembler, Uber driver, bulk coffee delivery driver, and shift manager at a popular sandwich shop that shall remain nameless. Because of this background, I tend to tell it like it is. I don't utilize vacuous political rhetoric or hide behind a façade of "objectivity." I side with the exploited and the oppressed, and if that makes me "biased," then so be it. I'm no elite political pundit or temporarily embarrassed millionaire, polishing the boot of the establishment for a shot at an MSNBC gig. I didn't get a full ride scholarship to Yale to study journalism because my father was in some macabre secret society. You've heard enough from people like that. But I still need to "sell myself," so here goes:

In these pages, I address some of the most controversial topics of our time, including white nationalism, police violence, U.S. foreign policy, Israel/Palestine, Venezuela, China, anti-fascism, Russiagate, Columbus Day, American exceptionalism, 9/11, and the legacy of Dr. Martin Luther King, Jr. This compilation of fiery political commentary also provides a compelling account of the Trump years unavailable through conventional media sources.

But wait! There's more! Are you wondering why a majority of Gen Z Americans hold negative views of capitalism[6] or why 70 percent of millennials say they would vote for a socialist?[7] Are you wondering how half of eligible voters can refuse to vote for either of the two viable political parties? Did you miss out on current events during the last four years and want to catch up?

If you are an anthropologist or a sociologist; an upper middle-class suburbanite or a member of either major political party; a bleeding-heart liberal or a baby leftist; a teacher or a learner; a descendant of apes or an intelligently designed being—then this book is for you.

This is a case study, a confession, a manifesto, an introduction to the Left, and an alternative history of the Trump era all in one. It is a relic of our time—a down-to-earth series of ramblings by a disgruntled, indebted millennial who blames all his problems on "neoliberalism" and now refers to himself as a "communist." It is a crucial text in our pursuit of understanding the current wave of radicalization that is disrupting these once "united" states. This author contends that, regardless of your orientation (political or otherwise), you will not regret reading this fine book.

Warnings and Considerations

Despite the humorous nature of the passages above, I felt the need to get serious for a moment. First, I would like to issue a general content warning for this book. Among other disturbing topics, the violence of war, conflict, and conquest is discussed from time to time in these pages (in graphic detail on a few occasions). Sexual assault and racism are also depicted on a few occasions. This might be unfortunate, but it is difficult to avoid due to the nature of the subjects I have covered.

The next topic I'd like to discuss briefly before you dive into this text is the high probability that, to some readers, the views expressed in this book may be perceived as offensive, insensitive, or even "Russian propaganda." It can be very painful to confront our deeply held beliefs, as I have personally discovered many times. But it can also be empowering. When I first got my hands on Howard Zinn's book *A People's History of the United States* shortly after high school, what ensued was both an epiphany and a catalyst. I suddenly became fascinated with history, sociology, politics, journalism, and the pursuit of knowledge more broadly. I was both baffled and enlightened to learn about the vast amounts of information that have been omitted or distorted regarding the conventional version of history we are told throughout our lives. But this process doesn't start and end with the way history is told; it often encompasses current events and many other important topics as well.

The truth is that the powerful have always used information warfare to benefit themselves and to entrench their power. This is something we must be aware of and push back against. There is a possibility that you, dear reader, will encounter claims or perspectives in this book that rub you the wrong way. All I ask is that you read with an open mind and investigate these topics for yourself. With all that being said, I truly hope you enjoy this book, and, most of all, I hope you gain something from it.

—*Matthew*

Part I

Part I serves as an introduction for those who are new to the Left.

This section establishes the general leftist political disposition and provides specific leftist perspectives on commonly discussed topics. The works featured here were written at different points during the aforementioned four-year period and are not in chronological order.

Part I

Part I serves as an introduction for those who are new to the Left.

Under Capitalism, a Pandemic Is a Time of Political Awakening

MARCH 2020

To say that the Trump administration responded inadequately to the COVID-19 pandemic would be a massive understatement. Trump's response was chock-full of misinformation,[8] racism,[9] dangerous proposals,[10] dangerous *policies*,[11] and a strain of conservative anti-intellectualism that ignores public health experts.[12] It has even been compared to former president Ronald Reagan's botched response to the AIDS epidemic in the 1980s.[13] This comparison also contains an important historical lesson: Reagan and Trump represent bookends of the American political tradition marked by deregulation, austerity, and corporate-funded governance (usually referred to as "neoliberalism").

Though many liberal pundits decry him as an uncharted divergence from "normalcy," Trump is simply the hideous, unmasked expression of neoliberalism—a ghastly gremlin our decaying society has vomited up after four decades of germination. In short, neoliberalism *created* Trump. Year after year we witnessed the bipartisan dismantling of labor unions, the passing of job-killing trade deals, the gutting of social services, the further corruption of political institutions, the continued stagnation of wages, and exorbitant expenditures on endless war. These developments tilled the political soil for an outgrowth of right-wing populism that attempts to hearken back to the "great" white supremacist legacy of America. It is a false populism that scapegoats immigrants and minorities, blaming the most marginalized for the societal rot produced by the implementation of "free market" ideology. Trumpism as a specific historical phenomenon is certainly new. But, in terms of the systemic nature of this barbarism, Trump is not an "aberration"—he is an inevitable extension of the existing system.

During the spread of the coronavirus and the subsequent economic crisis, Americans are learning the true nature of neoliberal disaster capitalism, or what journalist Naomi Klein has referred to as "Coronavirus Capitalism."[14] This current iteration is part of a disturbing historical trajectory. In short, corporate entities and powerful individuals have repeatedly exploited crises by swiftly implementing policies that further enrich the ruling class at the expense of everyone else—a phenomenon Klein has elucidated more broadly in her 2007 book *The Shock Doctrine: The Rise of Disaster Capitalism*.

As we are quickly realizing, the entire system is callous and predatory, and the tattered safety net that once existed is nowhere to be found. But, just like the virus itself, political consciousness is rapidly spreading. While seemingly undesirable jobs like cashiers, grocery stockers, and delivery drivers are proven to be essential by this crisis, it has also become evident that the captains of industry don't have any verifiable role other than extracting profit from our labor. As Jasmine Duff wrote in a recent *Hampton Institute* column, "these so-called wealth creators can spend months isolated in their mansions or country estates without this having any impact on the basic functioning of society."[15]

During a time of crisis, the wealthy can essentially hibernate in the midst of their vast resources. But to average workers, every dollar counts. Many will have to decide which bills to pay in order to leave enough money for groceries and other essentials. Because of this traumatic situation, the very *concept* of a student loan payment is being re-examined. People are realizing[16] that education should be a right, and that it is profoundly immoral to enslave college graduates with insurmountable debt simply for the crime of seeking knowledge to improve their life prospects. In times like these, the burgeoning student debt strike has the potential to gain significant momentum toward its ultimate goal of student debt cancellation and free public college.

In addition to the inherent injustices of the student debt crisis, our current pandemic is also laying bare the glaring inhumanity of a for-profit healthcare system. As Senator Bernie Sanders is fond of pointing out, the U.S. is the wealthiest country in the world, yet we are the only major industrialized country that doesn't guarantee healthcare as a human right. This "profit over people" mentality leads to tens of thousands of excess deaths and immeasurable suffering. But, when a deadly virus is expanding across the nation, these realities are magnified. When young people are dying of COVID-19 simply because they lack insurance,[17] and when people are continuing to work because they don't have guaranteed sick leave,[18] we begin to realize the terrifying truth of the old labor slogan "an injury to one is an injury to all."

* * *

During a pandemic that is exacerbated by neoliberal capitalism, people are quickly becoming radicalized. We are realizing that we don't actually *need* landlords, or bosses, or CEOs—these parasites that bleed the working class dry. They are, in other words, *non-essential*. In any civilized society, housing, healthcare, food, and education would be provided as prerequisites to the mere *concept* of justice. As Oscar Wilde once wrote, "The proper aim is to try and reconstruct society on such a basis that poverty will be impossible."[19] This means industrial production and technology should be directed toward meeting human need first and foremost. We are human beings, and our lives can no longer be commodified.

At this pivotal time, American workers are once again realizing the power of their labor and their strength in numbers. We're realizing that our participation is literally *essential* to the functionality of our society and that simply withholding our labor, our rent check, our student loan payment, can bring the entire system to its knees.

White Supremacy and Capitalism: The Two-Headed Dragon that Must Be Slain

AUGUST 2017

A four-decade onslaught of neoliberal Reaganomics has decimated the American working class. Median wages have remained stagnant since the late 1970s, despite a consistent increase in productivity. The top 1 percent owns nearly 40 percent[20] of the country's wealth, and top CEOs now take home more than 300 times that of the average worker (a 1,000 percent increase since 1978).[21] There are 40 million Americans officially living in poverty[22] and about 100 million more are struggling to afford basic necessities (but are not considered "poor" because the standard has not been adequately updated since the 1960s).[23] And keep in mind—this is happening in the richest country in the world. The vast majority of new income goes to the top 1 percent,[24] and *one family*—the Waltons of the Walmart empire—has more wealth than the bottom 40 percent of the population.[25]

Wealth concentration and poverty under neoliberalism aren't abstract concepts; they have tangible consequences. For example, half of all Americans don't even live paycheck to paycheck,[26] student loan debt is diminishing the prospects of home ownership,[27] climate change is beginning to devastate poor communities while helping the rich,[28] and 35,000 people die every year due to a lack of access to healthcare.[29]

But this is a democracy, right? Who would vote for such a grim existence? Well, according to an academic study from Cambridge, there is no correlation between public opinion and government policy.[30] Turns out the economic elites are running the show (a reality that was recently entrenched by the Citizens United ruling).

Generic, theoretical capitalism is inseparable from our current paradigm of advanced, hyper-consumerist, job-shipping, union-busting, soul-crushing neoliberalism. The capitalist class has fought tirelessly to achieve this sadistic system, which is the culmination of an evolutionary history of laissez-faire. Long ago, Adam Smith planted roses, but all that remain are the thorns. As Dr. Martin Luther King, Jr. once said, "today capitalism has out-lived its usefulness."[31]

But capitalism is not an equal opportunity destroyer. These social tragedies demonstrably and empirically affect folks of color at vastly disproportionate rates. For instance, the average net worth of Black households in the U.S. is $6,314, compared to $110,500 for the average white household.[32] Black Americans are more than twice as likely as white Americans to be poor,[33] and a white male with a criminal record is more likely to get a job than an equally qualified person of color with a clean record.[34] Median Black household income is approximately $43,300, while median white household income is around $71,300.[35] This discrepancy is roughly 40 percent greater today than it was in 1967. And these economic disparities are just the beginning.

In the realm of mass incarceration, more than 40 percent of American inmates are Black men, while that demographic only makes up 6.5 percent of the general population. In the realm of police violence, Black teens are *21 times* more likely to be shot and killed by the police than white teens.[36] These statistics could continue for pages. Profound systemic racism poisons every aspect of American society. These horrors are manifestations of the racial caste system that has always existed in the United States, a history that is discussed at length by Michelle Alexander in her book *The New Jim Crow: Mass Incarceration in the Age of Colorblindness*.

We often forget that merely six decades ago, our country maintained a government-sanctioned apartheid system. This included the intentional creation of Black ghettos[37] through redlining and other discriminatory policies. Political inertia, white backlash, and the racist War on Drugs have worked together to preserve the vestiges of white supremacy. The reality on the ground looks a lot like the same ol' Jim Crow; that guy we swore we kicked out in the 1960s.

But racism isn't just systemic; it is often overt. The recent emergence of Donald Trump as a political force made this crystal-clear.[38] Not only did the Ku Klux Klan[39] and white nationalists endorse him, but even for his voting base, "fear of diversity" was a significant motivating factor.[40]

The visceral evils of racism are clearly apparent, but what is seldom discussed is that these ideologies also serve to drive a wedge between working-class white folks and working-class people of color, distracting them from their true nemesis—the ruling capitalist class. This is a classic example of "divide and conquer," and has benefited the elites immensely. In this sense, racism is a byproduct of capitalist society. As Kwame Ture (also known as Stokely Carmichael) once observed, "Racism gets its power from capitalism. Thus, if you're anti-racist, whether you know it or not, you must be anti-capitalist. The power for racism, the power for sexism, comes from capitalism, not an attitude."[41]

We need to build a movement to confront and destroy this dual evil of racial and economic exploitation. And we need to stop being afraid of the "S" word.

* * *

Socialists have a rich tradition of fighting racism, from the Black Panther Party to the Communist Party of Alabama[42] to Cuba's crucial support for Black South Africans during Apartheid.[43] Socialists view racism as not only contrary to worker solidarity, but as a destructive and dehumanizing hierarchy, just like the class system itself. And indeed, capitalism and racism have enjoyed a symbiotic relationship thus far. Two modern organizations that are battling this double-headed beast are Democratic Socialists of America (DSA) and Redneck Revolt.

Founded in 1982, DSA is the largest socialist organization in the United States, with a total dues-paying membership of more than 92,000.[44] Members have been active in opposing the agenda of the Trump administration, as well as carrying the torch of the Bernie Sanders "political revolution." DSA has been on the front lines fighting for a $15 minimum wage, Medicare for All, LGBTQ equality, climate justice, reproductive rights, rent control, and many other progressive causes. However, one thing that separates DSA from other progressive organizations such as Our Revolution is its fervent anti-capitalism. As the DSA document *Where We Stand: Building the Next Left*[45] explained:

> We are socialists because we reject an international economic order sustained by private profit, alienated labor, race and gender discrimination, environmental destruction, and brutality and violence in defense of the status quo. We are socialists because we share a vision

of a humane international social order based both on democratic planning and market mechanisms to achieve equitable distribution of resources, meaningful work, a healthy environment, sustainable growth, gender and racial equality, and non-oppressive relationships.

On the topic of anti-racist activism, DSA Honorary Chair and prominent intellectual Cornel West wrote:

> A long and deep legacy of white supremacy has always arrested the development of U.S. democracy. [...] When the system is declining, it can bring despair. That's why Black Lives Matter—and all other young people of all colors who are mobilizing—is a beautiful thing. We are having a moral and spiritual awakening. It gives us democratic hope. [...] It's time to move from being spectators, to being actors.[46]

Members of Redneck Revolt are not liberals. They are pro-gun, pro-labor, anti-fascist, and anti-racist. The movement, which began in 2016 as an outgrowth of the John Brown Gun Club, has dozens of vetted chapters around the country. This diverse organization is rapidly expanding and focuses on recruiting rural Southern and Appalachian working-class folks to join the fight against white supremacy and capitalism while defending and supporting people of color and other marginalized communities. Many of these impoverished white folks have been voting against their own interests for decades after falling for the xenophobic rhetoric of prominent politicians. As founding member Dave Strano explained:

> The history of the white working class has been a history of being an exploited people. However, we've been an exploited people that further exploits other exploited people. While we've been living in tenements and slums for centuries, we've also been used by the rich to attack our neighbors, coworkers, and friends of different colors, religions and nationalities.[47]

Member Max Neely summarized their strategy by saying simply, "We use gun culture as a way to relate to people. No liberal elitism. Our basic message is: guns are fine, but racism is not."

* * *

White supremacy and capitalism have ravaged this country for far too long. They feed off one another and can be found at the root of myriad systemic injustices. Let's break this trend and democratize the economy, and society as a whole. Let's uproot and expose our vicious history of racism and dismantle the new Jim Crow. And to those of us with various forms of privilege, let's use it to fight for a better future for everyone.

5 Commonly Whitewashed Aspects of Dr. King's Life and Death

JANUARY 2019

Dr. Martin Luther King, Jr. was a Baptist minister, a brilliant orator, and a prolific civil rights leader who was assassinated in 1968 at age 39. Today he is primarily remembered for his "I Have a Dream" speech, his role in organizing the Montgomery bus boycott, and for receiving the Nobel Peace Prize in 1964. King's life of activism helped inspire the passage of historic racial justice legislation, including the Civil Rights Act of 1964, the Voting Rights Acts of 1965, and the Fair Housing Act of 1968.

Americans are taught that Dr. King was a popular and universally cherished leader. King, we are told, was charismatic, passionate, yet essentially non-political; he wanted to make the world a better place without rocking the boat too much. However, the Reverend Martin Luther King, Jr. was a complicated historical figure, and our collective understanding of his legacy is oversimplified. Here are five facts about Dr. King that are often omitted from conventional American discourse.

1. He often criticized American capitalism

In addition to his well-known battle against racism, Dr. King was a tireless advocate for economic justice.[48] He regularly worked with labor unions, and even wrote the introduction to a popular booklet that proposed a "second New Deal," which was distributed by prominent unions. King's economic vision largely stemmed from his religious faith and his belief in the "social gospel."

In his final speech to the Southern Christian Leadership Conference in 1967, King said,

> One day we must ask the question, 'Why are there forty million poor people in America?' When you ask that question, you begin to question the capitalistic economy.[49]

This wariness toward capitalism was not a late-in-life phenomenon.

Here are a few excerpts from a speech Dr. King gave in 1956:

> They tell me that one tenth of one percent of the population controls more than forty percent of the wealth. Oh America, how often have you taken necessities from the masses to give luxuries to the classes. If you are to be a truly Christian nation you must solve this problem.[50]

> You can work within the framework of democracy to bring about a better distribution of wealth. You can use your powerful economic resources to wipe poverty from the face of the earth. God never intended for one group of people to live in superfluous inordinate wealth, while others live in abject deadening poverty. God intends for all of his children to have the basic necessities of life, and he has left in this universe 'enough and to spare' for that purpose. So I call upon you to bridge the gulf between abject poverty and superfluous wealth.[51]

King's anti-capitalist stance can even be verified as early as 1952. That year, in a letter to his wife Coretta, Dr. King wrote, "I imagine you already know that I am much more socialistic in my economic theory than capitalistic. […] Today capitalism has outlived its usefulness."[52]

2. He was vehemently anti-war

The general public was first introduced to Dr. King's anti-war perspective in 1965, when he told reporters that "millions of dollars can be spent every day to hold troops in South Vietnam and our country cannot protect the rights of Negroes in Selma." During the following years, King continued to articulate his vision for peace, ultimately culminating in his 1967 "Beyond Vietnam" speech.[53] Here are several pertinent excerpts from that message, which King delivered on April 4, 1967 at Riverside Church in Harlem:

> As I have walked among the desperate, rejected, and angry young men, I have told them that Molotov cocktails

and rifles would not solve their problems. I have tried to offer them my deepest compassion while maintaining my conviction that social change comes most meaningfully through nonviolent action. But they asked, and rightly so, 'What about Vietnam?' They asked if our own nation wasn't using massive doses of violence to solve its problems, to bring about the changes it wanted. Their questions hit home, and I knew that I could never again raise my voice against the violence of the oppressed in the ghettos without having first spoken clearly to the greatest purveyor of violence in the world today: my own government.

They must see Americans as strange liberators. The Vietnamese people proclaimed their own independence in 1954 [...] after a combined French and Japanese occupation and before the communist revolution in China. They were led by Ho Chi Minh. Even though they quoted the American Declaration of Independence in their own document of freedom, we refused to recognize them. Instead, we decided to support France in its reconquest of her former colony. Our government felt then that the Vietnamese people were not ready for independence, and we again fell victim to the deadly Western arrogance that has poisoned the international atmosphere for so long.

So they go, primarily women and children and the aged. They watch as we poison their water, as we kill a million acres of their crops. They must weep as the bulldozers roar through their areas preparing to destroy the precious trees. They wander into the hospitals with at least twenty casualties from American firepower for one Vietcong-inflicted injury. So far we may have killed a million of them, mostly children.

The war in Vietnam is but a symptom of a far deeper malady within the American spirit, and if we ignore this sobering reality, we will find ourselves organizing 'clergy and laymen concerned' committees for the next generation. They will be concerned about Guatemala and Peru. They will be concerned about Thailand and Cambodia. They will be concerned about Mozambique and South Africa. We will be marching for these and a dozen other names and attending rallies without end unless there is a significant and profound change in American life and policy.

These are revolutionary times. All over the globe men are revolting against old systems of exploitation and oppression, and out of the wounds of a frail world, new systems of justice and equality are being born. The shirtless and barefoot people of the land are rising up as never before. The people who sat in darkness have seen a great light. We in the West must support these revolutions.

As was the case with his innate anti-capitalism, Dr. King did not suddenly begin opposing war later in life; "deep currents of anti-imperialism"[54] could be found in King's writings, even in those from his earlier days as a student. But this unconventional moral conviction proved even more detrimental to King's reputation than his critique of economic injustice.[55] In the aftermath of this infamous speech, one poll found that only nine percent of the general public sympathized with King's views on Vietnam.[56] Scores of Southern Christian Leadership Conference donors announced the withdrawal of their support, 168 newspapers denounced him, and President Johnson ended his formal relationship with King.[57]

3. He practiced armed self-defense

After white supremacists bombed his home in 1956,[58] King applied for a concealed handgun permit. Although the permit was ultimately denied, King still kept firearms in his home, and armed guards often protected King and his family. As journalist Adam Winkler explained, "one adviser, Glenn Smiley, described the King home as 'an arsenal.' William Worthy, a black reporter who covered the civil-rights movement, almost sat on a loaded gun in a living-room armchair during a visit to King's parsonage."[59]

Dr. King would eventually give up his guns and wholeheartedly embrace pacifism, but armed self-defense nevertheless played a central role in the civil rights movement. As author and civil rights activist Charles E. Cobb, Jr. explained:

> Consider the mid-20th century Southern Freedom Movement. People are often startled when I insist that guns helped make that movement possible, but guns were a routine part of Southern life. They helped put food on the table in poor rural communities. They were used to fend off night riders seeking to murder civil rights activists and their supporters. Indeed, few Southern homes—Black or White—were without guns.
>
> Guns were not the problem—but how they were used was critical. Klansmen and the like defended White supremacy through violence. Their actions were backed by state and local governments and largely ignored by the federal government. The armed resistance of local movement supporters was invaluable to the movement's survival. Groups such as the Deacons for Defense and Justice of Louisiana, formed to protect nonviolent workers of the Congress of Racial Equality (CORE), or the 'Black Guard' formed in Monroe, N.C., by NAACP leader Robert Williams, were consciously political, highly disciplined and visibly active in protecting movement activists. But their contributions are erased by a canon that defines the Movement as 'nonviolent.'[60]

4. The FBI monitored and threatened him

Conventional American discourse often mythologizes King as a hero who was universally beloved—even during his lifetime. The truth is that J. Edgar Hoover said he was "the most notorious liar in the country,"[61] President Johnson called him a "goddamn n----- preacher,"[62] and the

FBI spied on him and attempted to intimidate him.[63] A Gallup poll even found that 63 percent of Americans held a negative view of King in 1966 (*before* his "Beyond Vietnam" speech).[64] It turns out Dr. King's fervent denunciation of white supremacy, capitalism, and military aggression was perceived as a real threat to the political establishment and the prevailing social order.

One of the most shocking revelations on this topic is a document that became known as the "suicide letter." On November 21, 1964, the King household received a poorly written letter attempting to blackmail Dr. King with alleged secrets regarding his sex life.[65] The anonymous author employed a vitriolic tone, referring to King as "vile," "adulterous," "immoral," and, near the end, as an "evil, abnormal beast." The now infamous missive, which King correctly surmised was the work of Hoover's FBI, concluded with a thinly veiled invitation to suicide:

> King, there is only one thing left for you to do. You know what it is. You have just 34 days in which to do (this exact number has been selected for a specific reason, it has definite practical significant. You are done. There is but one way out for you. You better take it before your filthy, abnormal fraudulent self is bared to the nation.[66] (*sic*)

In short, this disgusting stunt was an attempt by the FBI to "neutralize" Dr. King. The agency's wish came true on April 4, 1968, when King was assassinated in Memphis, Tennessee.

5. King's family members do not believe James Earl Ray was the assassin[67,68]

Based on what we now know about the FBI's paranoid disdain for King's activism (as well as the U.S. government's coordinated assassination of Black Panther Party leader Fred Hampton),[69] it is certainly reasonable to question the official narrative surrounding King's death. In lieu of speculation, here is a summary of the facts:

» On April 4, 1968, Dr. King was in Memphis supporting

striking workers and preparing for an upcoming march. While standing on the balcony of his hotel room, King was shot in the neck just after 6:00 p.m. and pronounced dead about an hour later.

» After a ten-month international manhunt, James Earl Ray was found, arrested, and quickly confessed to the murder of King. Three days later, Ray changed his story, recanting his confession and insisting his lawyer had coerced him into taking the guilty plea. Nevertheless, he was sentenced to 99 years in prison.

» Due to the FBI's history of harassing and monitoring King, his family doubted the agency's objectivity (to say the least) as it led the investigation of King's assassination.

» In 1993, a man named Loyd Jowers claimed in a television interview that King's death had been the result of a conspiracy involving organized crime and the U.S. government, and that he had personally participated in this plot.

» In 1997, King's son Dexter visited James Earl Ray in prison to personally ask Ray if he had indeed killed King. Ray replied, "No, no, I didn't, no. But like I say, sometimes these questions are difficult to answer, and you have to make a personal evaluation."

» After this interaction between James Earl Ray and Dexter King, Coretta Scott King decided to file suit against Loyd Jowers. In the subsequent 1999 civil trial, the jury unanimously found Jowers (and unnamed others) culpable in King's murder. The hearing lasted four weeks and included the testimonies of 70 witnesses, although Jowers himself did not take the stand during the proceedings.

* * *

"The evils of capitalism are as real as the evils of militarism and evils of racism."
–Dr. King, 1967

The tendency to whitewash the bold statements and actions of Dr. King has become an American tradition. As history professor Thomas J. Sugrue put it, "there is probably no figure in recent American history whose memory is more distorted, whose message is more bowdlerized, whose powerful words are more drained of content than King."[70] Dr. Cornel West refers to this process as the "Santa Clausification" of King's legacy.

In addition to this widespread distortion through omission, there is also a history of reactionaries hijacking King's image and cherry-picking his words in attempt to claim him as one of their own.[71] For instance, in the wake of the recent NFL protests, a popular meme claimed that King "didn't take the knee in protest of the flag or the anthem, he took the knee in prayer to God."[72] This implies that Dr. King would have turned a blind eye to horrific systemic racism and police violence, and obediently saluted a flag that represents vicious imperialism abroad and neoliberal tyranny at home. This notion is, of course, patently ridiculous.

The truth is that Dr. Martin Luther King, Jr. was an uncompromising "social justice warrior" and a left-wing radical who defied the liberal establishment, abhorred military conquest, denounced capitalist exploitation, confronted white supremacy, and was ultimately murdered for these convictions. Were King alive today, he would be on the front lines of the Black Lives Matter movement, the anti-war movement, and the progressive political movement more broadly. We can begin to honor his legacy by simply admitting this.

6 Disturbing Aspects of American Policing

JUNE 2020

On May 25, a white Minneapolis police officer strangled George Floyd to death by forcefully kneeling against his neck for more than eight minutes, despite Floyd insisting he could not breathe and despite numerous warnings from the crowd that had gathered.[73] An independent autopsy concluded his death was "caused by asphyxia due to neck and back compression that led to a lack of blood flow to the brain."[74] Floyd, a Black male, met this tragic fate after simply being accused of using a counterfeit twenty-dollar bill at a local business. It is no exaggeration to describe this horrific incident, which was filmed in its entirety, as a public lynching.

In the wake of this ongoing racist police violence, protests erupted in Minneapolis and nationwide. Police met demonstrators and passersby[75] alike with a barrage of additional violence[76] including the use of rubber bullets, tear gas, and even ramming protesters with police vehicles. The officer who conducted the killing of George Floyd was later arrested, but only after extensive public pressure including all-out rebellions. Due to a widespread realization of these shocking injustices, Americans are now re-evaluating the role of policing in their communities. Here are six disturbing aspects of American policing that should be included in this long overdue public discourse.

1. Police are not legally obligated to protect you

Due to the ubiquitous "to serve and protect" slogan utilized by police departments nationwide, there exists a popular notion that protecting American citizens from harm is an official duty of the police. However, legally speaking, this isn't quite true. The 1989 Supreme Court case *DeShaney v. Winnebago County Department of Social Services* concluded that, in an instance in which government employees fail to protect someone from harm, it does not violate the U.S. Constitution.[77]

In his comments regarding this case, Chief Justice Rehnquist said, "Nothing in the language of the Due Process Clause itself requires the State to protect the life, liberty, and property of its citizens against invasion by private actors." Furthermore, the *DeShaney* decision has been cited in subsequent cases, such as *Castle Rock v. Gonzales* (2005), affirming that—from a constitutional perspective—the police have no mandate to protect American citizens.

2. Police officers lie under oath on a regular basis

Based on the findings of the Mollen Commission report, a 1994 *New York Times* article observed that, "New York City police officers often make false arrests, tamper with evidence and commit perjury on the witness stand..."[78] The practice of police perjury is so common that it has been given the nickname "testilying." Although the scope of this phenomenon is impossible to fully document, more than two dozen instances of police lying in court have emerged since 2015. These cases "are almost certainly only a fraction" of the total.[79]

Police officers have been caught lying about witnessing drug deals, about suspects carrying weapons, and have issued many other false allegations of criminal behavior. In addition to such blatant falsehoods, Baltimore police even "carried toy guns to plant on people they shot."[80] Furthermore, dishonest officers are seldom held accountable. "There's no fear of being caught," an NYPD officer told the *New York Times*. "You're not going to go to trial and nobody is going to be cross-examined."[81]

3. There is an epidemic of domestic abuse among police families

Regardless of one's personal views regarding American policing, the fact that our laws are regularly enforced through violent methods cannot be avoided. This "official" violence is unfortunately all too often supplemented with violence in the household. According to the National Center for Women and Policing:

Two studies have found that at least 40% of police officer families experience domestic violence, in contrast to 10% of families in the general population. A third study of older and more experienced officers found a rate of 24%, indicating that domestic violence is 2–4 times more common among police families than American families in general. A police department that has domestic violence offenders among its ranks will not effectively serve and protect victims in the community.[82]

Just like the problem of police perjury, shockingly little is done to address this devastating reality. As a *New York Times* piece concisely explained, "In many departments, an officer will automatically be fired for a positive marijuana test, but can stay on the job after abusing or battering a spouse."[83] The victims in these cases are uniquely vulnerable because the perpetrators have access to firearms, know the locations of women's shelters, and know how to manipulate the legal system to avoid penalty.[84]

Journalist Conor Friedersdorf summarized this issue by observing, "There is no more damaging perpetrator of domestic violence than a police officer, who harms his partner as profoundly as any abuser, and is then particularly ill-suited to helping victims of abuse in a culture where they are often afraid of coming forward. The evidence of a domestic-abuse problem in police departments around the United States is overwhelming."[85]

4. Police kill far more people than mass shooters each year[86]

We are still barely scratching the surface of understanding the prolific American tradition of deadly police force.[87] Mapping Police Violence[88] is a project that is trying to change that. The statistics this organization has compiled are shocking, especially when compared to those of other Western nations.[89] For instance, American police killed 1,099 people in the year 2019 alone. That same year, a mere *three people* were killed by police in the United Kingdom.[90]

In terms of the scope of deadly encounters with the police, the year 2019 wasn't an anomaly for the United States. Between 2013 and 2019,

American police officers killed 7,666 people—averaging 1,095 per year.[91] On top this already horrific reality, killer cops face criminal convictions in less than one percent of cases,[92] and prosecutors often add insult to injury by blaming and vilifying the victims.[93]

5. Local police departments have become heavily militarized

Journalist Dexter Filkins once observed that, in the aftermath of the 2013 Boston Marathon bombing, "the police in Boston and its suburbs sent armored cars into the streets and deployed officers dressed like Storm Troopers, who carried assault rifles and fanned out across neighborhoods as though they were in an infantry division in Afghanistan." Such surreal scenes exemplify a process that has been decades in the making. As sociology professor Alex Vitale explained in his book *The End of Policing*:

> U.S. police are armed with an amazing array of weapons from semiautomatic handguns and fully automatic AR15 rifles to grenade launchers and .50-caliber machine guns. Much of the militarized weaponry comes directly from the Pentagon through the 1033 Program, a weapons transfer program that began in 1997. This program has resulted in the distribution of $4 billion worth of equipment. Local police departments can get surplus armaments at no cost—with no questions asked about how they will be used. Small communities now have access to armored personnel carriers, assault rifles, grenade launchers, and a variety of 'less lethal' weaponry, such as rubber bullets and pepper-spray rounds. The Department of Homeland Security (DHS) has also given out $34 billion in 'terrorism grants,' a tremendous boon for military contractors trying to expand their reach into civilian policing markets.[94]

6. Slave patrols were one of the first forms of American policing

The racial element of American police violence is impossible to ignore. In recent years, the canonized, hashtagged names of various victims are painful reminders of the epidemic of state-sponsored terror against people of color. George Floyd, Philando Castile, Michael Brown, Eric Garner, Sandra Bland, and Breonna Taylor, however, are just the tip of this blood-drenched iceberg. For instance, *Newsone* has compiled a list of 89 Black men and boys who have recently been killed by American police officers.[95] But this gruesome phenomenon of violent, racialized policing is far from a recent development. In fact, as Professor Connie Hassett-Walker explained:

> Policing in southern slave-holding states had roots in slave patrols, squadrons made up of white volunteers empowered to use vigilante tactics to enforce laws related to slavery. They located and returned enslaved people who had escaped, crushed uprisings led by enslaved people and punished enslaved workers found or believed to have violated plantation rules. The first slave patrols arose in South Carolina in the early 1700s. As University of Georgia social work professor Michael A. Robinson has written, by the time John Adams became the second U.S. president, every state that had not yet abolished slavery had them. Members of slave patrols could forcefully enter anyone's home, regardless of their race or ethnicity, based on suspicions that they were sheltering people who had escaped bondage.[96]

From the time of the Reconstruction-era Black Codes[97] through the ostensible end of Jim Crow laws, the police enthusiastically and violently enforced the state's racial hierarchy. However, contrary to popular belief, this American iteration of apartheid didn't end in the 1960s with the passage of historic civil rights legislation. In the wake of the civil rights era, a new Jim Crow emerged in the form of the (still ongoing) War on Drugs, which a Nixon advisor later admitted was aimed at further disrupting the Black community.[98]

During the terror of the War on Drugs and the resulting mass incarceration of Black and Brown Americans, the police continued in their traditional role as the state's loyal foot soldiers in its pursuit of oppressive and racist objectives. The aforementioned systemic racism is compounded by the fact that "white supremacists and other domestic extremists maintain an active presence in U.S. police departments and other law enforcement agencies."[99] In short, throughout the entirety of American history, policing and white supremacy have been inextricably linked.

It's Time To Abolish Columbus Day

OCTOBER 2020

Columbus Day is one of the few U.S. federal holidays named after a specific historical figure. Christopher Columbus, the Italian explorer whom this holiday celebrates, is a name most Americans recognize. Growing up in the U.S. and attending public schools includes exposure to the customary narrative regarding Columbus—an account resembling a fairy tale or a mythology in which our main character is practically deified. We are told with great enthusiasm that Columbus not only "discovered America," but that he was an honorable, noble, brave, and talented explorer.

As children, we are forced to memorize the names of his ships: the Niña, the Pinta, and the Santa María. There are streets, schools, and even cities named after this supposed "hero." But the gruesome aspects of Columbus's legacy have—until quite recently—remained largely omitted from history textbooks and the mainstream narrative in the United States, which canonizes him as something comparable to a founding father.

The Real Columbus[100]

During his first voyage, Columbus sailed across the Atlantic, attempting to find an alternate trade route to Asia. He had used crafty public relations methods to convince King Ferdinand and Queen Isabella of Spain to fund his voyages. Columbus himself was seeking fortune and fame, while Spain was seeking a colonial empire. Therefore, Columbus and the Spanish authorities came to an agreement: Columbus would be allowed to govern over any territories he discovered and would be entitled to ten percent of the profits that resulted from this venture. Simply put, Columbus was looking for gold. However, since he was a fanatical and pious Christian, Columbus also saw this conquest as an opportunity to convert foreign peoples to Christianity.

Despite popular lore, Columbus was basically a con man. He had little knowledge of sailing or exploration, and in fact, his understanding was often inaccurate. As history professor Joel Helfrich explained:

> Educated Europeans believed the world was about

24,000 miles in circumference, meaning 10,000 miles separated Europe's west coast from Asia's east coast (too far to sail in the small ships of the time). Columbus, using his understanding of the Bible and other ancient sources, argued instead that the world was much smaller, and that Asia was only 3,000 miles away. In fact, his misunderstanding of geography motivated his voyage.[101]

Columbus proceeded to offer a large cash reward for the first crewmember to spot land (the equivalent of about $1,500 in modern currency). But when a man named Juan Rodrigo Bermejo spotted an island, Columbus rescinded the offer and claimed *he himself* had actually seen the island a few hours earlier. Columbus and his men first landed at what is now called the Bahamas, though they falsely believed they had arrived in India. They met the indigenous people (including the Arawak and the Taíno peoples) and mistakenly referred to them as "Indians."

Columbus wrote the following account of this initial encounter:

> They are the best people in the world and above all the gentlest—without knowledge of what is evil, nor do they murder or steal…they love their neighbors as themselves and they have the sweetest talk in the world…always laughing.

But what he wrote next revealed his true character and intentions:

> With fifty men we could subjugate them all and make them do whatever we want.

And that's exactly what he and his men proceeded to do. During their second voyage in 1495, after landing at what we now know as Haiti, Columbus and his men abducted 1,500 Arawak men, women, and children and took them as captives. Of these, 500 were put on the ships and forced into cages. Of those 500, only 300 survived the journey back to Spain where they would become slaves. This is recognized as the origins of the Trans-Atlantic slave trade, which is the true legacy of Christopher Columbus.

Indigenous people who were not transported back to Spain were forced to search for gold on the islands, and those who collected enough gold were given a copper token to wear around their necks. This signified that they had done their duty, so to speak. But this also meant that those who were later found without this token were punished.

Here are some disturbing examples of the sadistic brutality that ensued:

» Indigenous people who did not deliver enough gold had their hands cut off
» Those who ran away were hunted down by dogs
» Prisoners were burned to death
» Villages were raided
» Columbus's men raped indigenous women, who were often sold as sex slaves
» Indigenous people were dismembered simply so Columbus's men could test the sharpness of their swords
» The corpses of indigenous people were used as dog food

We are often told not to judge the past by the standards of the present. But the shocking violence of Columbus and his men was recognized even during this seemingly unimaginable era. Bartolome de las Casas, who was a Spanish priest at the time, wrote a first-hand account in which he opined, "What we have committed in the Indies stands out among the most unpardonable offenses ever committed against God and mankind and this trade [the enslavement of indigenous people] as one of the most unjust, evil and cruel among them."

In the subsequent years, this vicious venture amounted to genocide; de las Casas estimated that, in less than two decades, 3 million indigenous people had been killed or died due to the conditions of enslavement. In addition to the brutality, mass murder, and slavery, Columbus also fabricated reports of the resources he discovered on these voyages. He claimed to have found useful plants and products—misidentifying some and exaggerating the abundance of others. Knowing how absolutely sadistic, murderous, repulsive, vile, and even unprofessional this man was, some might find it strange that there is a federal holiday to commemorate him. To make a long story short, here is how Columbus Day came to be: A Catholic fraternal organization called The Knights of Columbus lobbied Congress in the 1930s to recognize Columbus Day. In the 1800s and early 1900s there was substantial xenophobia directed toward Italian immigrants, who were not yet perceived as "white." This effort was therefore partially motivated by a desire to frame Columbus—and by extension Italians—as having a crucial role in the foundation of America and thus improving the image of Italians in the eyes of other Americans. President Roosevelt was convinced to make a proclamation recognizing Columbus Day in 1937, but it didn't officially become a federal holiday until 1968.[102]

An Alternative to Columbus Day

Columbus's ghastly voyages to the Caribbean initiated global European colonialism, and with it came the ruthless enterprises of slavery and genocide that continued for centuries. Nevertheless, Columbus Day remains a federal holiday. Thankfully, this is beginning to change. In recent years, many cities around the U.S. have essentially abolished Columbus Day and recognized Indigenous Peoples' Day instead. These include Denver, Phoenix, St. Paul, Minneapolis, and Seattle, as well as the entire states of Alaska, New Mexico, South Dakota, and Vermont. This effort began in 1992, and was led by Native American groups in Berkeley, California, which is the city that first officially adopted Indigenous Peoples' Day as a holiday that same year.

The growing prevalence of Indigenous Peoples' Day is an important step toward Americans becoming more educated and knowledgeable regarding the horrifying realities of colonialism and white supremacy. This knowledge is also useful in recognizing how this legacy influences modern events, such as the rise of white nationalism and right-wing domestic terrorism. Broadly speaking, an openness toward confronting this troubling history is crucial in our road toward indigenous sovereignty and decolonization.

Columbus Day, a commemoration of brutal colonialism, slavery, and genocide, has only been on the books for five decades. It is time to abolish this abomination and embrace Indigenous Peoples' Day.

The 2001 Terrorist Attack on American Soil Wasn't the Only '9/11'

SEPTEMBER 2018

On the morning of September 11, 2001, four commercial airliners were hijacked by 19 members of the Salafi jihadist organization al-Qaeda. One plane was deliberately flown into the north tower of the World Trade Center complex in Manhattan, closely followed by another crashing into the south tower. About 30 minutes later, a third plane collided into the western wall of the Pentagon in Arlington County, Virginia. The fourth and final aircraft crashed in a field in Somerset County, Pennsylvania, killing everyone on board.

This unprecedented, coordinated attack resulted in a loss of nearly 3,000 lives, making it the deadliest act of terrorism in American history.

The 2001 terrorist attack on American soil was monstrous and tragic beyond words, but unfortunately it wasn't the first "9/11." On September 11, 1973, a CIA-backed military coup ousted Salvador Allende,[103] the democratically elected president of Chile, paving the way for two decades of brutal dictatorship under the rule of General Augusto Pinochet. More than 3,000 people were murdered by Pinochet's regime,[104] and more than 30,000 were tortured. During this tyranny, Chile was part of a broad network of Latin American despots and death squads known as Operation Condor, which was assisted by the CIA. This episode is but one example of violent U.S. hegemony that has contributed to global resentment and even blowback, such as the aforementioned terrorist attacks on September 11, 2001.

In a series of interviews published as a slim pamphlet shortly after that fateful day, famous linguist and political dissident Noam Chomsky discussed terrorism as a global phenomenon, including the Western double-standard regarding the term. By detailing an array of examples, such as Kosovo, Nicaragua, Lebanon, Iraq, Palestine, and Sudan, Chomsky observed that, based on the conventional definition of the word, the U.S. is a top global purveyor of terror. The immediate death, destruction, trauma, and misery caused by this vicious tactic is abhorrent, but this violence can also perpetuate itself, often continuing for generations. Regarding the 9/11 attacks and the origins of al-Qaeda specifically, Chomsky explained:

> The CIA did have a role, a major one in fact, but that was in the 1980s, when it joined Pakistani intelligence and others (Saudi Arabia, Britain, etc.) in recruiting, training, and arming the most extreme Islamic fundamentalists it could find to fight a 'Holy War' against the Russian invaders of Afghanistan.[105]

* * *

The term "blowback" was coined by the CIA to describe the unintended consequences of covert actions undertaken by the U.S. military and intelligence agencies.[106] The word was first used in this context during internal speculation after the agency helped overthrow the Iranian government in 1953 (summarized on page 48).

In his groundbreaking exposé[107] of said phenomenon, the late Chalmers Johnson vividly chronicled the far-reaching tentacles of the post-war American empire. He explained how this multifaceted hegemony causes profound resentment and hatred throughout the world, sometimes even leading to cases of blowback. Such incidents have included terrorist bombings against Americans abroad, with targets like U.S. embassies in Africa, a Pan Am flight above Lockerbie, Scotland, and an apartment building in Saudi Arabia that housed American soldiers. Blowback also includes organizations and foreign leaders who were once armed and/or supported by the U.S. later becoming enemies of the U.S., as was the case with the Mujahideen in Afghanistan. And the presence of roughly 700 American military bases in 130 different countries[108] only seems to fan these flames.

A post-9/11 manifestation of blowback was the formation of the gruesome terrorist organization known as ISIS,[109] which was only possible thanks to the U.S.-led invasion and occupation of Iraq.[110] Though ISIS committed shocking acts of violence, this outcome wasn't shocking at all; it was entirely predictable, based on the U.S. military's own research. In 2004, then-secretary of defense Donald Rumsfeld requested a report from the Defense Science Board Task Force regarding the efficacy of American policy in the Middle East. The task force's response included the following:

> American direct intervention in the Muslim World has paradoxically elevated the stature of and support for radical Islamists, while diminishing support for the U.S. to single-digits in some Arab societies.[...] In the eyes of Muslims, American occupation of Afghanistan and Iraq has not led to democracy there, but only more chaos and suffering. [...] Muslims do not 'hate our freedom,' but rather, they hate our policies.[111]

This unsavory, yet sober analysis of our incendiary role in foreign conflicts is often omitted from mainstream discourse because it is profoundly embarrassing to many prominent institutions and public officials. Acknowledging our own role in perpetuating mass violence calls into question the popular notions of American exceptionalism and American moral benevolence. Former President George W. Bush's explanation of the events of September 11, 2001 (which occurred early in his first term) revolved around the notion that "they hate our freedoms."[112] Bush's evaluation was vastly different from the words of the actual perpetrator, Osama bin Laden, who outlined his motives in a detailed "letter to America."[113] Though the missive is laced with Wahhabi rhetoric, it also elucidates bin Laden's political grievances, including verification that 9/11 should be categorized as "blowback."

Bin Laden's objections to U.S. policy included its support for the Israeli occupation of Palestine (including the killing of civilians and destruction of homes), its sanctions against Iraq (resulting in about half a million civilian deaths), its military bases throughout the Middle East (including in Saudi Arabia), its military actions in Somalia, and its support for regimes that have killed and oppressed Muslims throughout the world. Although this al-Qaeda kingpin was an extremist and a mass-murderer, his explanation certainly holds more water than Bush's glib retort.

* * *

The devastation caused by the 9/11 attacks inspired a beautiful outpouring of support and solidarity among people from all backgrounds coming together to assist and comfort one another. However, the aftermath of this atrocity also unleashed pervasive nationalism, ethnic and religious profiling, violations of constitutional rights, and imperialistic mass murder in the Middle East.

The 9/11 slogan became "Never Forget." As a nation, we certainly won't forget such a large-scale catastrophe, but in a sense, we also "Never Remember." Instead of starting the timeline only when an event affects us directly, we should analyze the historical context of such events and have the courage to look in the mirror and see our decades of relentless global violence, both covert and overt. We should also—as participants in a democracy—evaluate our role in the profound suffering, sorrow, resentment, and blowback these policies have generated.

The Korean War[114] may help put this in perspective: American military aggression in North Korea between 1950 and 1953 resulted in the equivalent of *hundreds* of 9/11s, based on the respective death tolls. The same is true of American aggression in Southeast Asia during the 1960s and '70s. In recent decades, the so-called "War on Terror" has taken well over a million lives. The scope of these blood-drenched foreign conquests, combined with consistent historic U.S. support for dictatorships and death squads, makes it easy to see why America is widely perceived as the greatest threat to world peace.[115]

On this harrowing anniversary, let's honor the victims of September 11, 2001 by remembering the victims of our own terrorism as well. If we change our ways, we can address the root causes of these conflicts, and prevent similar tragedies from occurring in the future. Let's acknowledge our history, confront our current complicity in mass murder,[116] [117] and work to end this cycle of violence.

Part II

Part II is essentially a history of the Trump era, as told by a leftist who lived through it (me).

It also contains a subplot during which I transition from a run-of-the-mill Bernie Bro into a hardcore, degenerate Marxist. Thanks, Obama. I mean Biden. Anyway, this section is structured in chronological order, based on the date each piece was completed.

Does the U.S. Government Really Care about Syrian Civilians?

APRIL 7, 2017

Last night, President Trump approved the bombing of targets inside Syria "in retaliation for the regime of Bashar Assad using nerve agents to attack his own people."[118] This chemical attack was an unspeakable atrocity, resulting in at least 70 civilian deaths.[119] Who can argue with the U.S. military's response?

Let's back up for a second. Was there actual evidence that the Syrian government was responsible for this attack? Or are we just supposed to blindly swallow U.S. government pronouncements like we did when they invaded Iraq in 2003 based on fabricated intelligence?[120]

After the devastating sarin nerve gas attack in August 2013 near Damascus, then-president Barack Obama immediately placed blame on Bashar al-Assad. But, as Pulitzer Prize-winning investigative journalist Seymour Hersh observed, the facts on the ground should have produced skepticism. In fact, it seemed more likely that the attack was carried out by a rebel group like al-Nusra (al-Qaeda's Syrian affiliate).[121]

So, what did the mainstream news media have to say about Trump's military aggression? As was the case with Iraq,[122] the *New York Times* operated as a subservient mouthpiece for unsubstantiated State Department talking points.[123]

I'm not saying Assad couldn't have done it; I'm just saying we shouldn't take the statements of government officials as gospel, especially considering their impressive record of lying to the American public (not to mention Trump himself lied at least 560 times during his presidential campaign alone).[124]

It is certainly possible that Assad is responsible for this gruesome crime. But when was the last time the U.S. military intervened in a foreign conflict for actual humanitarian purposes? And when was the last time a U.S. military intervention improved any situation? If one were to create a slogan for the U.S. invasion and occupation of Iraq, it would go something like this: "I spent trillions of dollars and killed hundreds of thousands of people, and all I got was this lousy ISIS."[125]

Speaking of Iraq, let's take a little trip down memory lane. In 1988, Iraqi president Saddam Hussein killed at least 3,200 people in a chemical weapons attack against Iran.[126] Despite this rampage, Hussein retained U.S. support until he invaded Kuwait in the summer of 1990. American officials were aware of this murderous plan in advance, yet helped their buddy out anyway.[127] In fact, Iraq had been using chemical weapons since 1980. Yeah, Saddam Hussein was totally our bro. We even provided him with intelligence and weapons during the aforementioned onslaught.[128]

Since the 1950s, the U.S. government has spent billions of dollars and incalculable additional resources installing and supporting dozens of brutal dictatorships, terrorist organizations, and death squads across the globe.[129] One of its first success stories was Iran. In 1953, the CIA coordinated with British intelligence to overthrow Mohammad Mosaddegh, the democratically elected prime minister. You see, Mosaddegh, supported by the Iranian people, had this wacky idea that the Iranian people should benefit from the oil that was located beneath their feet. So they nationalized the oil industry, kicking out the parasitic British corporation now known as BP. Naughty, naughty. After the coup,

Iran returned to its old-school monarchy days with the reinstatement of the Shah, who presided over a quarter-century of ruthless despotism. This is one of many cases that illustrates the U.S. government's deep and long-standing hostility toward the prospects for democracy and national sovereignty around the world. When the Iranian people decided to end this Western-imposed dictatorship by having a revolution in 1979, Uncle Sam said, "not cool," and hollered at his boy Saddam.[130][131]

If you still believe the U.S. cares about civilians in the Middle East, consider the fact that they've consistently supported Saudi Arabia for decades. The government of this Gulf ally consists of a brutal, theocratic monarchy recognized as having one of the worst human rights records in the world[132] and is known as the epicenter of the Wahhabi ideology behind terrorist organizations like ISIS and al-Qaeda.[133] The Saudi military is also currently bombing Yemen with billions of dollars worth of U.S. weapons, creating a humanitarian crisis rivaling that of Syria.[134]

Are we really expected to believe that the most massive military empire in human history gives a flying fuck about 70 Syrian civilians being killed in a chemical weapons attack? An empire that, by the way, has killed an estimated 1.3 million people (mostly civilians) just since the "War on Terror" was declared.[135] Give me a break. It may be difficult to pin-point the exact geo-strategic motivations for U.S. intervention in Syria, but if nothing else, this aggression will generate enormous profits for the junkies in the war industry, help maintain U.S. global dominance, and turn our population, once again, into a herd of flag-sucking nationalists.

Instead, let's think critically, rationally, and learn from our collective mistakes. Let's approach foreign policy cautiously, repudiating the knee-jerk reactions of white saviors and world police. After all, nothing promotes fascism like a good, old-fashioned war. In short, let's avoid giving Trump more power than he already has.

White Nationalist Terror and Anti-Fascist Resistance

AUGUST 2017[136]

On August 12, hundreds of American fascists gathered for a "Unite the Right" rally in Charlottesville, Virginia. The belligerent crowds exhibited Confederate and Nazi flags, red "MAGA" hats, and shouted racist chants like "blood and soil" while protesting the city's decision to remove a statue of Confederate general Robert E. Lee. The rally, which was halted by violent clashes before it officially began, was organized by former Daily Caller writer Jason Kessler and boasted an impressive line-up of prominent white supremacists who were slated to speak to the reactionary hordes.[137]

Suddenly, in a shocking act of domestic terrorism, a gray Dodge Challenger accelerated into a crowd of anti-racist counter-protesters, injuring 19 people and killing one. Details of this story are still emerging, but a suspect has been arrested and identified as 20-year-old James Alex Fields, Jr., a registered Republican[138] who was photographed holding a neo-Nazi Vanguard America shield and milling around with other basement-dwelling bigots.

The deceased victim of this gruesome tragedy was 32-year-old Heather Heyer, an anti-racist activist who gave her life fighting against fascism. Heyer is now a martyr and should be held in the highest regard for the sacrifice she made protecting our society, as should the other victims of this disgraceful and cowardly act of terror. The People must come together, not only to mourn this loss, but to organize and continue fighting racist, totalitarian movements that threaten our communities and our democracy.[139]

President Trump responded to these events by saying, "We condemn in the strongest possible terms this egregious display of hatred, bigotry and violence on many sides, on many sides."[140] Since he evidently didn't want to alienate members of his base, much less his administration, the president refused to describe the situation with accurate terms like "white supremacy" and "terrorism."

Right-wing terrorism is clearly a threat to American society,[141] just as it has been throughout our history, and we must confront it. We need to call it terrorism, call the perpetrators what they are—Nazis and white supremacists—and we need to stop using euphemistic language and double standards when describing the problem.[142] Ignoring white supremacy is like ignoring cancer; it will only continue to grow. We also need to organize, unite, and those of us who feel comfortable (especially if we're privileged) should become trained and armed for community defense. People of color, immigrants, religious minorities, and the LGBTQ community especially need support now.

The Paradox of Tolerance

A significant portion of the mainstream discourse on the "alt-right" revolves around the First Amendment. Racist right-wing groups often organize hate-filled rallies behind the veil of "free speech," and many centrists and liberals go along with this. While I believe it is generally important to support freedom of speech, I don't think hate-speech should be included in this "freedom." After all, hate-speech (including racist and xenophobic talking points) is a tactic fascists and right-wing activists use to fear-monger and pander to ignorant folks who may be susceptible to further radicalization. It also serves to threaten and terrorize people of color, minorities, immigrants, and other already marginalized groups. According to the Southern Poverty Law Center, there are currently more than 800 active hate groups in the United States.[143] The goal of these violent, reactionary movements, if history is any indication, is actually to inhibit free speech, diversity, and ultimately democracy itself.

Shutting down fascists in the streets is essential to preventing the rise of their movements. If possible, we should drown out their "free speech" with ours (although this seems less practical due to recent events). Black bloc[144] is another prominent tactic used by anti-fascists on the ground to deny a platform to neo-Nazis and other fascists (I witnessed the success of the black bloc first-hand at a counter-protest I attended shortly after Trump took power). It is our responsibility to confront hate-speech, xenophobia, homophobia, racism, nationalism, and other manifestations of fascism. When individuals or groups exhibit ideologies that have elements in common with fascism, it is cause for concern.

White nationalist guru Richard Spencer, for instance, has called for the ethnic cleansing of the U.S. to make way for a homogeneous white nation. History is clear that these types of movements have end goals of genocide, or, at best, a hyper-nationalistic society with a brutal apartheid system.

While I don't generally advocate censorship, I also don't think advocating "free speech" for genocidal fascists is tenable, especially if they are actively inciting violence against already marginalized groups and empowering terrorists (inciting violence is not protected under the First Amendment anyway). You might say I am "intolerant of intolerance." I believe this is the most practical position to hold when attempting to preserve the freedoms we purport to uphold in this society. Suffice it to say that it is easier to fight fascism when it has not yet seized power.

The following excerpt from Karl Popper's 1945 book *The Open Society and Its Enemies*[145] eloquently articulates this outlook:

> Less well known is the paradox of tolerance: Unlimited tolerance must lead to the disappearance of tolerance. If we extend unlimited tolerance even to those who are intolerant, if we are not prepared to defend a tolerant society against the onslaught of the intolerant, then the tolerant will be destroyed, and tolerance with them.—In this formulation, I do not imply, for instance, that we should always suppress the utterance of intolerant philosophies; as long as we can counter them by rational argument and keep them in check by public opinion, suppression would certainly be unwise. But we should claim the right to suppress them if necessary even by force; for it may easily turn out that they are not prepared to meet us on the level of rational argument, but begin by denouncing all argument; they may forbid their followers to listen to rational argument, because it is deceptive, and teach them to answer arguments by the use of their fists or pistols. We should therefore claim, in the name of tolerance, the right not to tolerate the intolerant. We should claim that any movement preaching intolerance places itself outside the law, and we should consider

incitement to intolerance and persecution as criminal, in the same way as we should consider incitement to murder, or to kidnapping, or to the revival of the slave trade, as criminal. (Popper, 1945, p. 581)

The Necessity of Antifascism

After two epic bloodbaths—the American Civil War and World War II—we still have yet to fully extinguish the poisonous ideologies of Nazism and white supremacy. As it currently stands, white nationalists and neo-Nazis are evidently comfortable marching down American streets, waving Nazi flags, shouting racist slogans, intimidating communities, and even murdering people who are fighting for a better world. Combatting this age-old enemy will involve a well-coordinated effort. For instance, the decentralized anarchist collective known as "antifa" (short for anti-fascist), which is primarily known for its street confrontations, also engages in intelligence gathering, doxing, and pressure tactics.[146] The movement got some good press recently after author and civil rights activist Dr. Cornel West, who participated in the counter-demonstration, said, "We would have been crushed like cockroaches if it were not for the anarchists and the anti-fascists. [...] They saved our lives, actually. We would have been completely crushed, and I'll never forget that."[147]

The roots of antifa can be traced back to 1930s Germany, when working-class organizations courageously fought Nazism under the now famous label "Antifaschistische Aktion."[148] Anti-fascism more broadly has been instrumental in liberation struggles around the world.[149] In mainstream discourse, there has often been a charge of "violence on both sides" when discussing antifa. Semantically, the term "violence" shouldn't even be used to describe anti-fascism, since the methods in question boil down to self and community defense. Antifa is a *response* to fascist violence. If a woman is sexually assaulted and defends herself by punching her attacker in the face, it wouldn't make sense to claim that "there was violence on both sides." One side is the *aggressor* and one side is the *victim* fighting against the original aggression. The notion of moral equivalence between these two parties—which has been advocated by Trump and others—is a disingenuous and insidious form of victim-blaming that, in the aforementioned context, further promotes fascist organizing and recruitment.

We should go further than simply condemning this logically and morally fallacious argument by actively supporting and promoting groups that seek to protect the vulnerable. For instance, two armed anti-fascist organizations that have recently emerged are Redneck Revolt and Socialist Rifle Association. The history of armed resistance in conjunction with non-violence is one of the many aspects of our history that we tend to omit or downplay. A great example is the untold story of how guns made the civil rights movement possible (see page 26). Force and pacifism can be used within the same struggle; they are not mutually exclusive. We're beginning to see an understanding of this, with some mainstream defense of antifa,[150] and I hope this trend continues. However, this is much bigger than just antifa and other related movements; it's about the concept of self-defense itself. Protecting one's family or community shouldn't just be a conservative talking point, but a human value that transcends partisan politics. Let's not only reclaim this concept from conservative monopoly, but expand it to include the fervent defense of people of color, LGBTQ individuals, minorities, immigrants, and other marginalized members of our communities, as Malcolm X said, "by any means necessary," including the defensive use of force.

As we should all now realize, political protests aren't just casual gatherings with friends. I don't pretend to have all the answers, but simply proclaiming "love trumps hate" has proven dangerously naïve. It seems that, going forward, we should strive to be well organized and intimately prepared to defend ourselves, our comrades, and our communities against right-wing terrorism. This prospect is certainly complex and will require myriad resources and solidarity among many groups and movements. But the discussion is long overdue. The battle against systemic racism and entrenched white supremacy is essential, but a prerequisite to this continued struggle is addressing the very real threat of physical violence.

New Prospects for the Left Amid Extreme Wealth Concentration

NOVEMBER 11, 2017

The Institute for Policy Studies recently released an important, yet disheartening report[151] on wealth concentration which found that the richest three Americans currently own more wealth than half of the population. Its additional findings paint a bleak picture of a burgeoning First World oligarchy:

> The billionaires who make up the full Forbes 400 list now own more wealth than the bottom 64 percent of the U.S. population, an estimated 80 million households or 204 million people—more people than the populations of Canada and Mexico combined.
>
> The median American family has a net worth of $80,000, excluding the family car. The Forbes 400 own more wealth than 33 million of these typical American families.
>
> One in five U.S. households, over 19 percent, have zero or negative net worth. 'Underwater households' make up an even higher share of households of color. Over 30 percent of black households and 27 percent of Latino households have zero or negative net worth to fall back on.

The authors of the report also observed that these statistics likely constitute a conservative estimate of the true scope of economic inequality, since "the growing use of offshore tax havens and legal trusts has made the concealing of assets more widespread than ever before."

In what seemed to be a direct response to this dire situation, progressives and socialists accomplished sweeping electoral victories throughout the U.S. on November 8.[152] These included the election of Larry Krasner (a civil-rights attorney and Black Lives Matter supporter) to the position of Philadelphia's District Attorney, the election of Seema

Singh Perez (an open socialist and Bernie Sanders supporter) to a seat on the Knoxville city council, and the election of Justin Fairfax (a progressive and environmentalist) to the position of Virginia's lieutenant governor. (Fairfax also became the second African American in Virginia's history to be elected to statewide office.)[153] In Maine, a Medicaid expansion referendum that was supported by Our Revolution was overwhelmingly passed by voters. Among the additional victories on the Left were 14 candidates who were endorsed by Democratic Socialists of America, an organization whose membership has quadrupled during the past year.

This leftward trend seems likely to continue into the future, if the attitudes of millennials are any indication of the trajectory of U.S. politics.[154] For instance, a recent YouGov poll found that 44 percent of millennials would like to live in a socialist country (42 percent favored a capitalist country). A 2014 poll conducted by libertarian think tank Reason-Rupe found that 58 percent of those between 18 and 24 years old have a positive view of socialism (56 percent viewed capitalism favorably).[155] And, while a 2016 Gallup poll did find a slightly higher preference for capitalism among millennials (57 percent, versus 55 percent for socialism), the results for these two options were within the poll's margin of error.[156]

Although millennials seem evenly divided between their espousal of capitalism and socialism, it's clear that this younger generation has a much more favorable view of socialism than baby boomers, who, as studies indicate, overwhelmingly support capitalism (only about one fourth viewed socialism positively). A concrete verification of this fact was the widespread millennial support for candidate Bernie Sanders—a self-described democratic socialist—during the 2016 presidential primaries (Sanders received more votes from those under age 30 than Trump and Clinton combined).[157]

* * *

One logistical issue that will have to be addressed is whether this progressive shift will take place with the cooperation of the Democratic Party establishment, or in spite of it. Aside from the fact that the Democratic National Committee (DNC) is inherently hostile toward democracy itself,[158] there have also been recent indications of vehement resistance to progressive change within the party. These include

Donna Brazile's revelations regarding the DNC's efforts to rig the 2016 presidential primaries in Clinton's favor,[159] as well as the purge of progressive Democrats by current DNC Chair Tom Perez.[160] Senator Bernie Sanders recently published a proposal for "fixing the Democratic Party,"[161] but many are wary of this prospect.

Regardless of the tactics, one thing remains certain: Grassroots political action will continue, because Americans are sick and tired of business as usual, which has resulted in half the population living in or near poverty,[162] tens of millions without access to healthcare, an uncontrollable student debt crisis, starvation wages, and other staggering systemic injustices. In the wealthiest country in world history, prioritizing dignity and prosperity for everyone is not only possible; it is a moral imperative.

Bipartisan Brutality Toward the People of El Salvador

JANUARY 16, 2018

Last week, the Trump administration said it would revoke the Temporary Protected Status (TPS) of more than 200,000 Salvadorans who live in the United States,[163] many of whom initially fled their home country due to a devastating series of earthquakes in 2001. Rescinding this protection would force immigrant families to leave the country by September 9, 2019, or possibly face deportation.

Defenders of this troubling policy decision claim the program is no longer necessary, but, based on Trump's recent "shithole countries" comments[164]—as well as his decades of flagrant racism and alliances with a vast assortment of bigots and fascists—it's clear that this policy is based on a disturbing white nationalist fantasy. The malevolent nature of this decision is not merely due to its attempt at small-scale ethnic cleansing; it's also crucial to recognize the immense danger Salvadorans would face by returning to their country of origin.

El Salvador is part of the "Northern Triangle," which also includes Honduras and Guatemala, and is one of the most violent and unstable regions in the world,[165] second only to actual war zones. Brutal criminal gangs such as MS-13 have gained power, and government security forces have implemented an "iron fist" policy of extrajudicial killings in gang-controlled areas.[166] Cora Currier and Natalie Keyssar of *The Intercept* explained how poverty-stricken youth are often trapped between gangs and government forces:

> Kids in El Salvador face well-documented threats at the hands of gangs, from extortion to forced recruitment as members or 'girlfriends' of members. Being a witness to a gang murder, or just being in the wrong part of town or on the wrong bus line, can get you killed. Increasingly, they also face violence from police. Poor youth are rounded up on suspicion of being gang members, hassled, imprisoned,

and, in some cases, killed. Shakedowns and cellphone seizures are common. Activists say police regularly plant evidence and rely on flimsy allegations of gang affiliation. Beyond physical violence, there is widespread economic and social stigma against people from areas where gangs have a robust presence.[167]

The moral gymnastics one must perform to justify forcing hundreds of thousands of people into such an environment is astounding. Indeed, there are many cases in which deportation can be a death sentence.[168]

This is undoubtedly an unfathomably hellish prospect and it must be stopped. But let's not hop on the "all bad things started with Trump" bandwagon too quickly. El Salvador-based journalist Hilary Goodfriend recently noted that the cancellation of TPS for Salvadorans is "just the latest injustice they've suffered at the hands of the U.S. state."[169] As Benjamin Schwarz of *The Atlantic* wrote, "What is indisputable is that for a decade American policymakers in Washington and American civilian and military personnel in El Salvador consorted with murderers and sadists."[170]

Before elaborating upon U.S. crimes against the people of El Salvador specifically, it's worth mentioning that the U.S. government, often covertly, had been supporting dictatorships and death squads throughout Latin America since 1954, when the CIA staged a coup to overthrow Jacobo Árbenz, the democratically elected president of Guatemala, primarily on behalf of United Fruit Company.[171]

In 1980, with standard Cold War dogma as justification, the brutal Salvadoran regime began receiving American military aid from none other than liberal icon Jimmy Carter. During the previous year, the Salvadoran military and associated death squads had murdered some 8,000 civilians—including four American churchwomen[172]—so it was clear from the outset that defeating the leftist Farabundo Martí Front for National Liberation (FMLN) was more important than even a vague concern for human rights.

In December of 1981, U.S.-trained Salvadoran military units arrived in a remote village called El Mozote.[173] They were searching for guerrilla fighters but found only village residents and peasants seeking safe haven.

Soldiers proceeded to round up the men—separating them from the women and children—and engaged in interrogations, torture, and mass executions. Soon after, these government forces took the women and older girls, raped them, and slaughtered them with machine gun fire. The soldiers concluded their massacre by butchering the remaining children and burning the village to the ground. In the end, approximately 1,000 civilians had been murdered.

As the years passed and the carnage continued, there was much deliberation among U.S. government officials regarding the continued support for the Salvadoran regime. But at the heart of this sinister alliance was a fanatical bipartisan belief that such a horrific bloodbath was necessary to serve American "national security interests." As Dr. Martin Luther King, Jr. once said, "Human beings cannot continue to do wrong without eventually reaching out for some thin rationalization to clothe an obvious wrong in the beautiful garments of righteousness."[174] By the time a peace agreement was reached in 1992, approximately 75,000 Salvadorans had been killed.[175] The United Nations estimated that about 85 percent of the civilian deaths had occurred at the hands of government forces and the associated death squads.

* * *

In the short term, vehement opposition toward Trump and his abhorrent policies is essential. We must defeat Trumpism, and the ideologies of white supremacy along with it. But in the long term, we also need to end these barbaric, imperialistic U.S. interventions around the world. Both of these legacies are based on colonial domination and Western chauvinism. Trump's white nationalism and liberal interventionism are indeed cut from the same cloth. Both need to be dismantled in order to build a world where liberty and justice aren't just buzzwords, but a reality.

On Russiagate

FEBRUARY 3, 2018

On October 7, 2016, unnamed U.S. intelligence officials claimed to be "confident that the Russian Government directed the recent compromises of e-mails from U.S. persons and institutions, including from U.S. political organizations."[176] Immediately, as I recall, the barrage of government statements was regarded as gospel by the liberal wing of the mainstream news media.

The certainty in this narrative is likely unwarranted, especially considering where it's coming from. Over the years and decades, U.S. intelligence officials have lied about WMD in Iraq,[177] domestic surveillance,[178] torture,[179] rendition,[180] Iran-Contra,[181] hiring Nazi scientists,[182] testing LSD on unwitting victims,[183] and, as previously mentioned, supporting a broad array of dictators, death squads, terrorists, and drug cartels throughout the world. The default government retort to those who mention these topics usually revolves around "protecting national security." But regardless of any flimsy justification for their crimes against humanity, the only reasonable response to statements made by the U.S. intelligence community should be firm skepticism.

Indeed, much of the substance of this real-life spy thriller for liberals has turned out to be sensationalistic and unfounded. For instance, the so-called Steele dossier was an instant classic among Democrats. But this document was developed by the Democrat-funded opposition research firm Fusion GPS and is full of errors and uncorroborated claims.[184] The January 2017 intelligence report made headlines as well. But, as *The Atlantic* noted, "it does not or cannot provide evidence for its assertions."[185] *The Washington Post* published a story about how Russia disseminated massive amounts of "fake news" during the 2016 U.S. presidential election. But it turned out to be false. They published another about Russian hackers penetrating the U.S. electric grid. That one turned out to be false as well.[186]

Such retractions weren't rare; three CNN journalists even resigned in shame after "an internal investigation by CNN management found that some standard editorial processes were not followed" in their publication of a story about a Russian investment fund that was later retracted.[187]

But that debacle didn't stop the network from hyping up another false story several months later.[188] Rather than alleged "collusion" between the Trump campaign and the Kremlin, the Russiagate story started being about journalistic malpractice,[189] partisanship, and paranoia.

Here we are, 15 months after the election, with four indictments[190] in the Trump-Russia probe, and evidence for the central Russiagate narrative is still as elusive as ever.[191] And yet a dogmatic belief in the original conspiracy theory persists, elevating Russiagate to the status of a faith-based religion for conventional American liberals and Democratic Party loyalists.

But liberals and Democrats believe in science. They must care about evidence, right? Why are these folks so obsessed[192] with the notion that Trump and Putin are working together to undermine the American electoral process when there's no supporting evidence? The answer is much more simple than any of the Russiagate hyperbole we've been subjected to. When Hillary Clinton, who seemed to be a presidential shoe-in, lost the 2016 election to an overtly racist real estate mogul, the Democratic establishment desperately needed an explanation. Or, better yet, an *excuse*. As journalist Aaron Maté explained:

> Recognizing this absence of evidence helps examine what has been substituted in its place. *Shattered*, the insider account of the Clinton campaign, reports that 'in the days after the election, Hillary declined to take responsibility for her own loss.' Instead, one source recounted, aides were ordered 'to make sure all these narratives get spun the right way.' Within 24 hours of Clinton's concession speech, top officials gathered 'to engineer the case that the election wasn't entirely on the up-and-up. [...] Already, Russian hacking was the centerpiece of the argument.[193]

The prospect of a foreign power hijacking American democracy might be terrifying, but apparently not as terrifying as looking in the mirror. If members of the Democratic Party establishment engaged in self-reflection, they would realize their complicity in our epidemic of wealth concentration and the devastation of the working class through neoliberal economics, their complicity in grave racial injustices and human rights violations through the War on Drugs and mass incarceration, and their responsibility for the 2008 financial crisis due to the repeal of Glass–Steagall under President Bill Clinton. All of these policies have painfully chipped away at the tiny speck of the "American Dream" that once remained. Reflection would also cause the leaders of the "blue team" to realize their complicity in imperialistic and unjustifiable wars of aggression that have left millions dead and wrought unfathomable destruction across the globe.

Clinton apologists constantly bragged about Hillary's "qualifications" during that fateful 2016 presidential campaign. When this sentiment is stripped of its euphemistic nature, it ends up simply meaning that this celebrated and accomplished politician would be an efficient conduit for the wholesale destruction of various nations—including our own. For those whose standard of living had consistently declined, decade after decade, at the hands of the neoliberal Washington consensus, the aforementioned prospect was extraordinarily easy to vote against. The American people didn't need a foreign boogeyman; the true enemy had been in their midst all along.

***

Evidence-based inquiry is the hallmark of human progress. It is the basis for the scientific method, the foundation of historical analysis, and it should play a central role in politics as well. When we engage in large-scale wishful thinking, confirmation bias, and evidence-free belief, we unwittingly step into the realm of creationists and climate change deniers, and that's dangerous territory. In addition to being a distraction from Trump's actual crimes, the Russiagate narrative is indeed proving to be influential in bellicose U.S. foreign policy (particularly regarding the Russia/Ukraine conflict).[194]

If we believe in Russiagate without evidence, what's to stop us from blindly swallowing the next unfounded justifications for war? We should recall that about 43 percent of congressional Democrats voted for the 2003 invasion of Iraq,[195] [196] which turned out to be justified with fabricated intelligence. Russia hysteria is developing into a new Cold War at a time when the Doomsday Clock has been moved to two minutes before midnight.[197] The ominous threat of nuclear annihilation seems to represent an increasingly possible scenario. A consistent demand for evidence is not only a crucial tool in developing a more complete understanding of reality; it may also be necessary for survival.

Trump's Muslim Ban Has Nothing to Do With National Security

JUNE 28, 2018

In a five-to-four vote, the U.S. Supreme Court has upheld the Trump administration's ban on travel[198] from five Muslim-majority countries (Syria, Iran, Yemen, Libya, and Somalia) and two countries that have been historically uncooperative with the U.S. empire (North Korea and Venezuela).

In her inspiring and heartfelt dissent,[199] Justice Sonia Sotomayor compared the ban to *Korematsu v. United States*, the Supreme Court decision that justified the internment of approximately 120,000 Japanese-Americans during World War II.[200] Regarding the ruling, Trump's White House stated, "It is the President's sacred duty to take action to ensure that those seeking to enter our country will not harm the American people."[201]

However, as journalist Mehdi Hasan pointed out in a recent episode of Deconstructed, "the number of Americans killed on U.S. soil by citizens from countries on the banned list is exactly zero."[202]

One prominent Muslim-majority country that didn't make the list is Saudi Arabia. This oil-rich monarchy is not only the single largest exporter of the ultra-conservative Wahhabi ideology behind terrorist organizations like ISIS and al-Qaeda, but many Saudi individuals and organizations were also culpable in the largest terrorist attack on U.S. soil. As journalist Branko Marcetic explained:

> Fifteen of the nineteen [9/11] hijackers were Saudi nationals, and the attack was planned by a scion of one of the country's wealthiest and politically connected families. The hijackers, we now know thanks to the release of twenty-eight previously classified pages from the 9/11 commission's report, had ties to members of the Saudi government, including the Saudi ambassador to the United States, who also belongs to the country's royal family. [...] Intelligence services suspect various Saudi charities of

funding extremists, including the Al Haramain Islamic Foundation. [...] Moreover, multiple members of the 9/11 commission have said they believe Saudi officials were involved in the attack.[203]

The Saudi government has also armed Salafi jihadists in Syria[204] and is currently conducting a large-scale bombing campaign against the defenseless, poverty-stricken population of Yemen. This is on top of the cholera epidemic that has recently ravaged the country, and some say this vicious military aggression may be reaching genocidal proportions.[205]

Based on clear threats posed from within its borders, you'd think Trump would be wary of the aforementioned Gulf monarchy, right? Think again. After the president's gleeful little trip to Saudi Arabia last year, he proposed a $500 million weapons sale to the kingdom (part of a $110 billion package),[206] which narrowly passed the Senate soon after his return.[207]

* * *

The notion that Donald J. Trump cares about the safety and security of Americans is laughable. With the corporate news media's relentless barrage of Russiagate hysteria, it's easy to briefly forget the troubling white nationalist nature of Trump's rise to power.

For instance, Donald Trump kicked off his presidential campaign by calling Mexican immigrants "rapists." He continued his reactionary and callous crusade by consistently advocating political violence[208] (including thinly-veiled nods to assassination),[209] mocking a disabled journalist,[210] and insulting the family of a deceased Muslim-American veteran.[211] He would later promote Islamophobic propaganda from the neo-fascist, anti-immigrant organization known as "Britain First."[212]

Trump's affinity for white supremacists[213] and his endorsement of neo-Nazis[214] emboldened the perpetrators of hate crimes.[215] He has employed racists,[216] white nationalists,[217] a man with links to Nazis,[218] and was endorsed by the Ku Klux Klan.[219] He even went on to devise an apparently Hitler-inspired program to document the supposed crimes of immigrants,[220] leading to the further demonization of an already marginalized and oppressed demographic. In short, Trumpism is largely based on white nationalism and "fear of diversity."[221]

A window into this vile worldview is the story of Steve Bannon and *The Camp of the Saints*. Bannon, Trump's former chief strategist and architect of the Muslim travel ban, often used the aforementioned French novel as a metaphor for his geopolitical concerns. Bannon's "alt-right" (i.e. white nationalist) news outlet *Breitbart* has also referenced the book, whose narrative involves hordes of Indian barbarians migrating to Europe to initiate the end of Western (i.e. white) civilization. As Paul Blumenthal and J.M. Rieger of *Huffington Post* explained:

> The white Christian world is on the brink of destruction, the novel suggests, because these black and brown people are more fertile and more numerous, while the West has lost that necessary belief in its own cultural and racial superiority.[222]

Stanford professor Cécile Alduy said the book is "racist in the literal sense of the term. It uses race as the main characterization of characters," and Republican commentator Linda Chavez called it "shockingly racist." *The Camp of the Saints* has been published various times in the U.S., and was usually funded, promoted, and celebrated by the anti-immigration movement and even advocates of population control like the pro-eugenics Pioneer Fund.

* * *

Trump's travel ban is a vicious and draconian policy based entirely on racial hatred and xenophobia. It has nothing to do with national security and everything to do with the neo-fascist desire to make America more "white." If we want to ban people, let's start by banning racists from positions of power. Let's ban white supremacists and fascists who put children in cages and fantasize about ethnic cleansing. Let's abolish ICE, overturn this outrageous travel ban, and make bigotry an impeachable offense.

It's Time for Progressives to Boycott Israel

NOVEMBER 15, 2018

Rashida Tlaib, Ilhan Omar, and Alexandria Ocasio-Cortez are among the recently-elected members of Congress who will soon head to Washington after historic victories. After unseating ten-term incumbent Joe Crowley of New York's 14th congressional district, Ocasio-Cortez became the youngest woman ever elected to Congress.[223] Rashida Tlaib (a Palestinian-American) and Ilhan Omar (a Somali-American) became the first Muslim congresswomen.[224] Ocasio-Cortez and Tlaib are also members of Democratic Socialists of America, the largest socialist organization in the U.S.[225]

In addition to their trailblazing achievements, these inspiring women of color share an extremely rare stance in American politics: concern for Palestinian human rights.[226] This view is so unheard of that most prominent left-leaning politicians could accurately be labeled "progressive except for Palestine."[227] A recent embodiment of this concept was the Texas senatorial candidate Beto O'Rourke. In an email correspondence, a member of O'Rourke's campaign staff wrote:

> Beto is a proud advocate of Israel. He believes that Israel is critically important to the United States, because it is the home of the Jewish people, because it is an exemplary democracy that shares our values, and because it is a crucial contributor to our national security objectives in the region.[228]

On the topic, a *Jerusalem Post* article added, "O'Rourke has consistently supported a strong U.S.-Israel relationship, and he has the voting record to prove it."[229]

What's wrong with supporting Israel?

For starters, the Israeli military routinely slaughters civilians who are trapped in an open-air prison known as the Gaza Strip.[230] This barbarism is often accomplished using billions of dollars in U.S. "foreign aid."[231] In its most recent massacre, the Israeli Defense Forces (IDF) killed more than 110 Palestinians, including 14 children, and injured more than 3,700 with live ammunition.[232] During these unimaginable atrocities, *one* Israeli soldier reportedly sustained "light injuries."[233]

The "Great March of Return" began on March 30, 2018, and involved almost exclusively peacefully protests to confront Israel's siege of Gaza, which began in 2006. However, the Israeli government attempted to justify its murderous assault by concocting various myths about the protests, including the claim that there were "violent mass incidents."[234] According to an Amnesty International report, "In most of the fatal cases […], some victims were shot from behind and in the upper body, including the head and the chest. Eyewitness testimonies, video and photographic evidence suggest that many were deliberately killed or injured while posing no immediate threat to the Israeli soldiers."[235]

In addition to the staggering death toll, the report added that "many have suffered extreme bone and tissue damage, as well as large exit wounds measuring between 10 and 15mm, and will likely face further complications, infections and some form of physical disability—such as paralysis or amputation." According to the Palestinian Health Ministry in Gaza, 2,200 people suffered leg injuries, 17 of which resulted in amputation.[236]

As Jewish academic Norman Finkelstein has noted, any use of force by Israel against the people of Gaza—in addition to being senseless and sadistic—is completely illegal under international law.[237]

Those unfamiliar with the dire situation in Gaza may find it strange that thousands are willing to risk life and limb simply to participate in political demonstrations. A 37-year-old Gazan woman elucidated this phenomenon by writing:

> Israel has been holding Gaza under blockade for more than ten years. Some of the young people participating in the protests and being wounded or even killed by soldiers, do not know what it's like to have running water and a steady supply of electricity. They have never left Gaza and grew up in a prison. You can't visit us; Israel doesn't allow anyone

to see what's going on here. There is no real life in Gaza. The whole place is clinically dead. The younger generations are crushed by the hopelessness and death everywhere. The protests have given us all a spark of hope. They are our attempt to cry out to the world that it must wake up, that there are people here fighting for their most basic rights, which they are entitled to fulfill. We deserve to live, too.[238]

How did this all start?

Without getting into the complex history of Zionism,[239] this conflict essentially began during the formation of the State of Israel. As Phyllis Bennis explained in her book,[240] *Understanding the Palestinian-Israeli Conflict*:

> When the British ended their Palestine Mandate in 1947, they turned control over to the United Nations. The U.N. Partition Agreement […] divided Palestine into sectors: 55 percent for a Jewish state and 45 percent for a Palestinian Arab state, with Jerusalem to be left under international control […] (Bennis, 2019, p. 12)

> When Israel was created as a state in 1948, 750,000 indigenous Palestinians, whose families had lived in Palestine for hundreds of years, were forcibly expelled by, or fled in terror of, the powerful militias that would soon become the army of the State of Israel. […] Despite international law and specific U.N. resolutions, none of those forced into exile have been allowed to return. (Bennis, 2019, p. 10)

> "In the 1967 war, Israel took over the West Bank, Gaza, and East Jerusalem, the last 22 percent of historic Palestine. Those areas are now identified as the occupied territories." (Bennis, 2019, p. 14)

Seven decades later, Palestinians still make up one of the world's largest refugee populations, with an estimated 6 million displaced.[241] In addition to the initial horrors of the Nakba[242] and the aforementioned mass murder in Gaza, Israel has implemented apartheid policies[243] and built an array of illegal colonial settlements in the West Bank. In this occupied region, Palestinians live with segregated roads and buses, Arab-only military checkpoints, discriminatory distribution of water and other resources, forced evictions, and frequent home demolitions.

Aside from consistent U.S. support, this ruthless occupation is also allowed to continue due to the systematic dehumanization of Arabs throughout Israeli society. School children are bombarded with negative stereotypes of Arabs and Palestinians in their textbooks, which often depict them as "bloodthirsty," "tribal," and "inferior."[244]

In a survey conducted by Israeli writer and researcher Adir Cohen, "seventy five percent of the children described the 'Arab' as a murderer, one who kidnaps children, a criminal and a terrorist. Eighty percent said they saw the Arab as someone dirty with a terrifying face." Regarding popular Israeli children's books, Cohen found that "sixty six percent […] refer to Arabs as violent; 52 percent as evil; 37 percent as liars; 31 percent as greedy; 28 percent as two-faced; 27 percent as traitors."

This blatantly racist indoctrination persists into adulthood, as evidenced by the delusional and hateful views of common Israelis[245] and the genocidal rhetoric of Israeli law-makers.[246]

How can we work to end Israeli military aggression and apartheid?

When most people hear the term "apartheid," they think of South Africa. South African Apartheid was a brutal racial caste system that began in 1948 and was finally dismantled in the early 1990s. One of the key strategies in bringing an end to this injustice was an international divestment movement involving universities, companies, governments, and other organizations around the world.

On July 9, 2005, Palestinian civil society organizations called for similar measures aimed at ending the Israeli iteration of apartheid (along with its other human rights violations and war crimes).[247] Specifically, this effort demands that Israel comply with international law by:

1. Ending its occupation and colonization of all Arab lands and dismantling the Wall
2. Recognizing the fundamental rights of the Arab-Palestinian citizens of Israel to full equality
3. Respecting, protecting and promoting the rights of Palestinian refugees to return to their homes and properties as stipulated in UN Resolution 194

This movement, which is called Boycott, Divestment, and Sanctions (BDS), has grown significantly in recent years,[248] and now includes academic and cultural boycotts. Prominent political organizations like Democratic Socialists of America and Jewish Voice for Peace have endorsed BDS, and even cultural icons like Natalie Portman and Lana Del Rey have inadvertently participated.[249] [250] This effort is certainly gaining momentum, but we have a long way to go.

The truth is that Israel is a flagrantly genocidal,[251] settler-colonial apartheid state that has murdered thousands and displaced millions. These horrific crimes have been committed with American weaponry, funding, and political complicity. Our freshman class of congresswomen is therefore very encouraging and may pave the way to a change in the narrative, and in turn, a change in our policies.

The Palestinian people can't wait; it's time we heed their call.

The 'Resistance' Cheers for Assange's Arrest

APRIL 11, 2019

Early this morning, WikiLeaks founder Julian Assange was forcibly dragged out of the Ecuadorian embassy in London by British police officers. According to Assange's lawyer Jen Robinson, the purpose of the arrest was "not just for breach of bail conditions but also in relation to a U.S. extradition request."[252]

Robinson also observed that "this precedent means that any journalist can be extradited for prosecution in the United States for having published truthful information about the United States."[253] The information Robinson is referring to is a cache of videos and diplomatic cables leaked by whistleblower and former Army intelligence analyst Chelsea Manning in 2010.

The leaks, which became known as the Iraq War Logs, exposed the visceral barbarism of American combat operations in Iraq between 2004 and 2009.[254] A video given the title "Collateral Murder" is the most well-known single item in this collection. The shocking footage was taken from a U.S. Apache helicopter during a strike on alleged insurgents in 2007. The crew members can be heard laughing and taunting their victims as a van of unarmed Iraqis arrives on the scene, attempting to help the injured. The crew then begins sadistically shelling the vehicle, wounding two children inside. In total, the strike killed a dozen people; two were Reuters journalists.[255]

As detailed throughout this book, the aforementioned carnage was not an isolated incident. In the sinister Orwellian protocol of modern times, those responsible for these unspeakable crimes walk free, while those who expose them are prosecuted.

You'd think the slaughter of journalists and a subsequent cover-up would make waves in the press. You'd think this story would be about the illegal acts exposed, not those exposing them. But why question the U.S. empire when defense contractors advertise on your networks?[256] And why hold government officials accountable when they are often primary sources for your stories? In capitalist countries like the United States, news is simply a business. The news companies[257] want to maximize profit and the government wants to conceal its crimes. With the advent of neoliberalism, government interests and corporate interests are often one in the same.

It's becoming crystal-clear to more and more Americans every day that the wealthy Washington punditocracy simply represents the interests of the state and the ruling class. In addition to being bootlicking lapdogs of the elite, prominent "news" personalities lack the spine to articulate even mild opposition to the political establishment and its blood-drenched history. Their relationship to the spooks of the intelligence community[258] and the mass-murderers of the military[259] is purely symbiotic. They are obedient, subservient cowards and stenographers for state power. If you don't toe the line on U.S. foreign policy, it could cost you your career, as people like Marc Lamont Hill[260] and Phil Donahue[261] have discovered.

The same "Resistance" media figures and politicians that denounced Trump's previous attacks on the press now sit idly by, either making jokes[262] or actively cheering, while a journalist is being prosecuted for publishing accurate and important information. As journalist Nathan Robinson explained:

> There has been plenty of over-the-top gloating about Assange's arrest. In the Atlantic, Michael Weiss said Assange 'got what he deserved'. Some Democratic politicians have been salivating at the possibility of prosecuting him. Hillary Clinton said that Assange needs to 'answer for what he has done'. Charles Schumer said he hoped Assange 'will soon be held to account for his meddling in our elections on behalf of Putin and the Russian government'. Dianne Feinstein has been calling for Assange to be brought here and prosecuted since 2010. The West Virginia Democratic senator Joe Manchin went even further, with the truly disturbing comment that 'now [Assange is] our property and we can get the facts and truth from him'.[263]

The so-called "Resistance" has shown unequivocally that their ostensible opposition to Trump has always been superficial. They spent the last three years wearing tinfoil hats, foaming at the mouth, and promoting McCarthyite conspiracy theories when they could have been engaging in actual journalism and tangible opposition. They cheered when Trump bombed Syria,[264] when he sponsored a coup attempt in Venezuela,[265] and now they're cheering for his most brazen attack on press freedom. If the self-proclaimed "Resistance" supports their opponent's most bellicose acts, what is their "resistance" worth?

* * *

This isn't about whether you think Julian Assange is a nice guy, or whether you think he's guilty of other unrelated crimes he has been accused of. This is about freedom of the press—a constitutional right and an essential attribute of a free society. This is about the right to challenge those in power when that power is abused. It's about standing up against imperialism and war crimes. It's about the prospects for democracy itself.

The arrest of Julian Assange sets a dangerous precedent for the future of journalism. If you consider yourself a journalist, a citizen, or simply a conscious human being who values the free exchange of information, please raise your voice in opposition to this flagrant authoritarianism.

The Ballot and the Bullet: Building Socialism in 'America's Backyard'

OCTOBER 21, 2019

When faced with momentous external challenges—be they colonialism, imperialism, or natural disasters[266]—the Cuban people have consistently risen to the occasion. In response to ongoing internal challenges, the popular new Cuban constitution (which took effect in April)[267] entrenches the solid Marxist-Leninist foundation of the island's socialist state while updating the 1976 constitution to better reflect the modern post-Cold War period.

Under the new constitution, each presidential term is five years, with a limit of two consecutive terms in office for those who serve. In addition, the role of Head of State is divided between the president and the newly established office of prime minister.[268]

Other new rights and policies include the presumption of innocence in criminal cases, the right to legal counsel, and the (heavily regulated) use of private property and foreign investment[269] to stimulate the economy (particularly to offset the revenue lost as a result of the continued U.S. blockade).

Despite the many exciting modernizations articulated by this fresh new document,[270] much remains the same. Cuba's Communist Party is still the only political party legally allowed to operate, and the state continues to control the land and means of production. The news media cannot be privatized, and, according to the new Magna Carta, Cuba will never return to the exploitative, pre-revolutionary capitalist system.

Bourgeois historians and pundits often glibly frame successful socialist governments as "authoritarian." But from a Marxist perspective, the proletarian state serves to protect the achievements of the revolution—including universal healthcare, education, housing, subsidized food, and land reform—from reactionary and imperialist threats (such as the CIA-backed coup Ernesto "Che" Guevara witnessed in Guatemala prior to the Cuban Revolution). In addition to recognizing the Communist Party's general success, apologists for Western capitalism should be compelled to grapple with the fact that significant democratic processes are occurring within Cuba's one-party system.

The process to draft a new constitution began in August of 2018 and included the input of millions of Cuban citizens.²⁷¹ Assemblies throughout the island were established, and thousands of "standard proposals" were debated for three months. In all, the old constitution faced 760 modifications. The proposed constitution was then featured in a referendum that took place on February 24, 2019. With massive voter turnout, the new constitution was easily passed when about 86 percent voted "yes."²⁷²

Based on the long-standing solidarity between Cuba and its Latin American ally Venezuela, this recent constitutional process undertaken by the Caribbean nation may have been partially inspired by Venezuela's ongoing Bolivarian Revolution. After the 1998 election of the popular Venezuelan revolutionary Hugo Chávez, the formerly discarded masses were not only lifted out of poverty, but politically empowered through a nation-wide upsurge in grassroots democracy.²⁷³

As historian Greg Grandin wrote in 2013:

> Chávez's social base was diverse and heterodox, what social scientists in the 1990s began to celebrate as 'new social movements,' distinct from established trade unions and peasant organizations vertically linked to—and subordinated to—political parties or populist leaders: neighborhood councils; urban and rural homesteaders, feminists, gay and lesbian rights organizations, economic justice activists, environmental coalitions; breakaway unions and the like. It's these organizations, in Venezuela and elsewhere throughout the region, that have over the last few decades done heroic work in democratizing society, in giving citizens venues to survive the extremes of neoliberalism and to fight against further depredations, turning Latin America into one of the last global bastion of the Enlightenment left.²⁷⁴

Shortly after Chávez was inaugurated, Venezuelan citizens voted to replace their 1961 constitution with a new document that "expanded the rights of all Venezuelans, formally recognized the rights and privileges of historically marginalized groups, reorganized government institutions and powers, and highlighted the government's responsibility in working towards participatory democracy and social justice."[275] This Bolivarian constitution includes mechanisms by which the document can be revised by the people through nation-wide participatory democracy. In 2007, for example, a series of constitutional reforms were debated for 47 days at more than 9,000 public events before a referendum finally took place.

* * *

At the height of the American civil rights movement, charismatic Black liberation leader Malcolm X issued a powerful ultimatum—"*the ballot or the bullet*"—in his famous 1964 speech. The metaphor of the proverbial "ballot" and "bullet" can be useful in recognizing both the political and the physical dimensions of socialist struggle. A historical example of these two seemingly disparate themes merging was the short-lived alliance between Chile ("the ballot") and Cuba ("the bullet") in the early 1970s, iconically symbolized when revolutionary leader Fidel Castro gifted a personalized AK-47 to democratically elected socialist president Salvador Allende.

But movements do not have to choose between these two options exclusively. Broadly speaking, Venezuela's revolution emerged through the ballot box and was later upheld through armed defense, whereas Cuba's revolution was itself an armed struggle that would later evolve through ballot initiatives and grassroots democracy.

The ongoing Cuban and Venezuelan revolutions are impressive enough by themselves, but the material conditions they arose from and the hardships they have endured make them utterly awe-inspiring. Unfortunately, socialism doesn't develop in a vacuum. It doesn't grow in a petri dish. Building international socialism brings with it the baggage of constant imperialist assaults aimed at exploiting labor and extracting resources on behalf of global capital.

Now a spectre is haunting Washington—the spectre of the Monroe Doctrine. In its belligerent re-imagining of the 19th century foreign policy staple, the Trump administration has demonized and attacked the sovereignty of both Cuba and Venezuela. In conjunction with a new round of economic sanctions against the so-called "troika of tyranny," former National Security Advisor and Bush-era war criminal John Bolton claimed last April that the "Monroe Doctrine is alive and well."[276]

Bolton also announced that the U.S. would reintroduce the Helms-Burton Act—a 1996 law that allows American citizens to file claims related to properties that were nationalized after the Cuban Revolution. However, as Dr. Arturo Lopez-Levy opined, "It is not the United States government's responsibility or place to force the [...] Cuban government to prioritize compensating Cuban right-wing exiles over demands for other reparations, such as for slavery or any of the many other abuses committed in Cuban history before or after 1959."[277] Furthermore, as author Saul Landau observed, "By 1991, [...] the Castro government had settled claims with most of the nations whose properties it had confiscated and offered terms to U.S. companies as well."[278]

In addition, the Trump administration began restricting U.S. travel to the island in June and revived the half-century-long economic blockade that was briefly loosened under the Obama administration. These Cold War-inspired policies are certainly draconian, but it seems the U.S. regime's primary target is Cuba's oil-rich ally across the Caribbean Sea. As Bolton himself admitted, "It will make a big difference to the United States economically if we could have American oil companies really invest in and produce the oil capabilities in Venezuela."[279]

After winning the Venezuelan presidential election on May 20, 2018,[280] Nicolás Maduro was sworn in on January 10, 2019 to begin his second term in office. Then, on January 22, Juan Guaidó—a man whom 81 percent of Venezuelans had never heard of—suddenly declared himself "interim president."[281] Although Guaidó did not run in any presidential election, American politicians and pundits quickly praised this brazen U.S.-backed coup attempt, some even insisting "this is our backyard!"[282] Washington's latest[283] regime-change effort in the Bolivarian Republic has thus far failed, but the Trump administration's brutal economic sanctions have killed an estimated 40,000 Venezuelans in just one year.[284]

Despite this rampant imperialism, there have been notable solidarity efforts—both between Cuba and Venezuela as well as internationally.[285] [286] [287] However, in its overall capacity for both relevant material analysis and tangible solidarity, the U.S. Left has gone astray. Steve Stiffler contends that the U.S. Left's failure to properly frame Chavismo allowed right-wing propaganda to gain control of the narrative.[288] This defeat in the realm of discourse led not only to the empowerment of far-right forces on the ground in Venezuela, but to a diminishment of the once reliable socialist support from within the empire.

An indispensable historical model we should look to for guidance is the Venceremos Brigade. In 1969, a group of young American radicals volunteered their manual labor to assist with Cuba's sugar harvest in the wake of the crippling U.S. embargo. This primary delegation to the island included 216 brigadistas who helped cut sugar cane for six weeks. Since then, the Venceremos ("we shall overcome") Brigade spearheaded solidarity efforts between Americans and Cubans, bringing in more than 10,000 people to engage in agricultural work, construction, and other projects. Former brigadista Diana Block recently recounted, "I had traveled to Cuba with the Venceremos Brigade in 1977. At that time many radical U.S. political organizations looked to Cuba, and other global anti-colonial struggles, for inspiration and direction. Following Cuba's lead, international solidarity was recognized as a key organizing principle."[289]

* * *

During my brief trip to Havana last summer I visited Museo de la Revolución. Located in the former presidential palace which had once housed U.S.-backed dictator Fulgencio Batista, this space had been transformed into a museum commemorating the Cuban Revolution and was undergoing renovation. A sizable mural of Fidel speaking to a crowd rested against a banister as workers on scaffolds applied a fresh coat of paint to the neighboring room. After examining the intriguing exhibits, I browsed the items in the gift shop and came across a concise booklet entitled *Notes on Che Guevara's Ideas on Pedagogy* by Linda Martí, Ph.D. In it, Martí emphasized the role of a humanistic philosophy in socialist society:

> Is humanism present in every daily decision made by every citizen of our country? Is this concept of a humanist conscience the basis of every analysis made of services, production, or education? Collectivism, as a new personality trait and an expression of humanism in interpersonal relations, was the object of study, inquiry, and experimentation of Che's theory and praxis."

Humanism—in an internationalist sense—can motivate the more privileged Western leftists among us to stand in solidarity with independent socialist projects of the Global South and denounce the neo-colonialist machinations of the ruling classes. Our struggle, after all, is global. Whether utilizing the ballot, the bullet, or both, we should work toward the liberation of all people and consign Eurocentric rubbish like the Monroe Doctrine to the dustbin of history.

A Journalist Was Arrested and the Mainstream Media Was Silent

NOVEMBER 3, 2019

It is somewhat rare to receive news that the author of the book you're currently reading has been arrested. But I recently learned that Max Blumenthal, investigative journalist and author of *The Management of Savagery*, was arrested by Washington D.C. police on the morning of October 25, 2019.

In a SWAT-style raid, Blumenthal's residence was surrounded by local police, some of whom threatened to break down his door. The arrest warrant listed him as "armed and dangerous"—a comically absurd claim clearly meant to elicit an intimidating response by law enforcement. After a dangerous ride in the back of a squad car, the author was subjected to 36 hours of detainment and denied access to legal counsel. Blumenthal recounted the details of this draconian incident in subsequent interviews.[290] [291]

The charge—simple assault—was based on a five-month-old warrant (which was initially rejected and later revived without Blumenthal's knowledge)[292] related to an attempt to deliver food to the besieged Venezuelan embassy.[293] Specifically, right-wing Venezuelan opposition activist Naylet Pacheco accused Blumenthal of kicking her in the stomach in an alleged incident on May 7, 2019.[294]

Blumenthal wholeheartedly denies this charge, referring to it as "fabricated" and a "malicious lie."[295] Furthermore, Blumenthal believes this targeting is an act of political persecution due to his adversarial investigative reporting. "It is clearly part of a campaign of political persecution designed to silence me and *The Grayzone* for our factual journalism exposing the deceptions, corruption and violence of the far-right Venezuelan opposition," Blumenthal stated.

In the wake of a recent U.S.-backed coup attempt, supporters and members of the right-wing Venezuelan political opposition engaged in an illegal siege of the Venezuelan embassy in Washington D.C.[296] Their vicious violence, racism, and sexism was well documented,[297] which makes this sensational charge leveled against Blumenthal seem like pure projection.

In an October 28 statement, the National Lawyers Guild International Committee (NLGIC) strongly condemned the arrest of Max Blumenthal. After providing an overview of the case, NLGIC joined the journalist "in noting that his arrest took place hours after *The Grayzone* issued a report on USAID funding to lobbyists for the Venezuelan opposition." The statement continued by observing that the arrest "appears to be a form of retaliation practiced against both embassy protection activists and critical journalists for their opposition to the U.S.' unlawful intervention in Venezuela, support for an attempted coup and unilateral coercive economic sanctions directed against the country."[298]

As journalist Joe Emersberger noted, the press and relevant NGOs have largely ignored this "troubling encroachment on freedom of the press."[299] In the Trump era, when "Resistance" Democrats constantly clamor about "authoritarianism" and "attacks on the press," you'd think the mainstream media would at least mention this chilling episode. But a quick online search confirmed a ubiquitous silence from the Fourth Estate.

From an idealistic ethical perspective, the refusal to report this injustice might seem baffling. But the mainstream corporate news media is simply a multi-billion dollar industry selling a product ("the news") for a profit. A concern for upholding the First Amendment's "freedom of the press" isn't part of the equation. Furthermore, as famous linguist and political dissident Noam Chomsky once wrote, "those who occupy managerial positions in the media, or gain status within them as commentators, belong to the same privileged elites, and might be expected to share the perceptions, aspirations, and attitudes of their associates, reflecting their own class interests as well."[300]

In addition to the inherently corrupting effects of the profit motive and the class solidarity of elite institutions in general, major news outlets often flagrantly collaborate with the U.S. military and intelligence community instead of reporting in the public interest. This has been true for decades, but as journalist Rania Khalek recently pointed out, a disturbing trend has emerged in which numerous former intelligence officials have been hired as political pundits by popular news outlets.[301] Even when these multi-millionaire news anchors aren't directly regurgitating the pronouncements of government officials, they still consistently cheer for covert and overt foreign interventions.[302]

In most cases, reporting that challenges the national security state narrative is either vilified or ignored, regardless of how accurate it is. This is why the prolific journalism of Max Blumenthal is so important. Over the years, Max has explored the dark side of U.S. foreign policy, from its imperialism in Latin America, to its arming of jihadists in Syria and Libya, to its complicity in Israeli war crimes. Blumenthal provides a perspective that is absolutely necessary—a robust challenge to the bipartisan consensus on endless war—and, in the wake of this obscene political persecution, should be vehemently supported and defended by anyone who believes in a free press.

Impeachment is a Ruling-Class Spectacle

DECEMBER 19, 2019

It is unquestionably good for American society and the well-being of common people to rid ourselves of the Trump administration. Donald Trump is a xenophobic, racist, sexist, nationalistic con man and a pathological liar. He is corrupt to his very bones and should never have been afforded a position of power over a single individual. His administration has perpetrated grave crimes, including child separation policies, operating concentration camps, arming the genocidal Saudi regime, giving the wealthy a trillion-dollar tax cut, implementing a "Muslim ban," and empowering white supremacists and domestic terrorists.

But Trump was not impeached for any of these crimes. The recent House of Representatives impeachment proceedings[303] primarily revolved around allegations that the president leveraged military aid to Ukraine in attempt to open politically-motivated investigations (never mind that some of this "aid" has reached the neo-Nazi Azov Battalion).[304]

In a sense, Trump's impeachment follows a historical pattern. Like Trump, former president Bill Clinton was impeached in the House of Representatives. As a teenager at the time, I recall being quite enthralled while perusing the salacious details of the Starr Report in my local newspaper. To be frank, Clinton was impeached primarily over an extramarital affair. Not for killing hundreds of thousands of civilians in Iraq through economic sanctions.[305] Not for bombing a pharmaceutical plant in Sudan,[306] likely leading to thousands of unnecessary deaths. Not for his expansion of the racist War on Drugs and the continued mass incarceration of Black and Brown Americans. Not for deregulating Wall Street with his repeal of the Glass-Steagall Act.[307]

William Jefferson Clinton was impeached for lying about a blow job.

Why weren't presidents like Clinton and Trump impeached for their most monstrous offenses? Why aren't presidents impeached for their austerity measures and assaults on the working class? For their overt violence against the poor and marginalized? For the bombs they drop or the terrorists they arm? Simply put, these flagrant crimes are part of the bipartisan consensus. They constitute a continuation of the policies of previous administrations—policies that were designed by and for the ruling class. Impeachment proceedings result from superficial feuds between the two major ruling class political organizations—the Democrats and the Republicans.

In the country that is known for exporting "democracy," politics is merely a spectator sport. A 2014 study from Cambridge even found that "majorities of the American public actually have little influence over the policies our government adopts."[308] Whether it's the popular Russiagate conspiracy theory, the latest missile strike against a disobedient nation, or the recent impeachment proceedings, the elite want you to feel like you're watching "Game of Thrones" or "House of Cards." They want you to feel that rush of dopamine, like when your favorite sports team prevails, even though your material conditions remain static and insufficient.

It is certainly reasonable to celebrate this historic event. Trump is only the third American president to be successfully impeached in the House. But it's also important to see the bigger picture. Even in the unlikely event that impeachment passes in the Senate, we'd still be left with the rotten neoliberal system that created Trump in the first place.[309] True "resistance" should seek to replace this barbaric system and create a government that works for all of us—not just the one percent.

Why I'm Voting for Bernie Sanders

JANUARY 4, 2020

If you've ever listened to the coarse, Brooklyn-accented voice of Senator Bernard Sanders for more than 30 seconds, you're probably aware of some troubling statistics regarding the ongoing four-decade decline in the American standard of living. For example, almost 80 percent of American workers live paycheck-to-paycheck,[310] 35,000 Americans die each year due to lack of access to healthcare,[311] 500,000 Americans are bankrupted by medical bills each year,[312] 44 percent of Americans can't afford a $400 emergency,[313] 45 million Americans[314] are burdened with a cumulative $1.7 trillion[315] in student loan debt, and, on a related note, about 40,000 senior citizens have their Social Security benefits garnished.[316]

In the wealthiest country in modern history, these facts should be shocking. But just in case you've grown accustomed to them, here are a few more harsh realities: Americans are taking Ubers to emergency rooms instead of ambulances.[317] They're traveling to Canada to buy the insulin they can't afford in the U.S. (where it is ten times the cost).[318] Millions of Americans are being poisoned by lead-contaminated water[319] (Flint is just the tip of the iceberg). The white/Black racial wealth gap is ten to one.[320] Oh, and slave labor is still a thing.[321]

Despite these appalling circumstances, certain people are actually doing quite well. While wages have been stagnant for the last four decades[322] (despite a consistent increase in productivity),[323] the top one percent has increased its share of the pie dramatically, now owning 40 percent of the wealth and receiving more than 90 percent of all new income in recent years.[324] This ongoing process of wealth concentration is no accident; it is an outcome of specific policies that accelerated in the late 1970s.

This new era was characterized by mass incarceration (powered by the disastrous War on Drugs), an obliteration of social programs, a historic decline in the prominence of labor unions, a mass-outsourcing of American jobs, and unfettered corporate hegemony—notably in the realm of political lobbying and campaign contributions. The Clinton administration's 1999 repeal of the Glass-Steagall Act set the stage for a dark climax in this age of austerity—the financial crisis of 2008. In the United States, this global catastrophe resulted in about 8.7 million Americans losing their jobs and as many as 10 million losing their homes.[325]

Such bleak observations aren't merely academic; for me, they're personal (as I mentioned in the preface). To paraphrase Bernie, if we can afford to bail out the white-collar criminals on Wall Street who destroyed our economy, I believe we can also afford to "bail out" the floundering working class. Bold solutions like Medicare for All, student debt cancellation, tuition-free public college, and publicly-financed elections were widely perceived as utopian pipe dreams during the 2016 presidential primaries when they initially entered public consciousness. But, much to the chagrin of the political establishment, Bernie's stubborn humanism has essentially set the policy agenda for the 2020 Democratic primaries (in no small part because these proposals now enjoy broad popular support).[326]

Sanders vs. Warren

This brand of rapid social progress is admittedly not for everyone. If you just want a "return to normalcy" and generally supported the Obama-era status quo, then you have a slew of candidates to choose from, including Biden, Buttigieg, and Bloomberg. But if you consider yourself a true progressive—if you, for instance, believe healthcare should be a human right, or if you, as Alexandria Ocasio-Cortez says, believe no one should be too poor to live—then I must address the elephant in the room: Why choose Bernie Sanders over Elizabeth Warren? After all, aren't their respective policy positions "almost indistinguishable"?[327] Contrary to popular belief, there are substantial differences between the policies, voting records, strategies, and overarching philosophies of Sanders and Warren. Let's go through some of the simple ones[328] first:

» Warren voted to approve Ben Carson as Secretary of Housing and Urban Development (Sanders did not).
» Sanders has a plan to eliminate *all* medical debt (Warren does not).

- » Sanders has a plan to eliminate *all* student loan debt (Warren has a plan to eliminate *most* student loan debt).
- » Warren voted for Trump's military budget increase in 2017[329] (Sanders did not).
- » Warren has been inconsistent on Medicare for All, and her more recent plan[330] even puts it on the back burner (Sanders has been consistent for decades).

Now let's dig a little deeper and explore the philosophical and strategic differences between these two prominent progressives. I believe these distinctions can be encapsulated by the fact that Sanders refers to himself as a "democratic socialist," whereas Warren has said, "I am a capitalist to my bones."[331] Furthermore, Elizabeth Warren's accidental campaign slogan became "I have a plan for that,"[332] whereas Bernie's is "Not Me, Us." Warren believes that the current system could use a few technocratic tweaks to make it less barbaric, while Sanders believes we need a massive, multiracial, grassroots, working-class movement to completely overhaul said system.

Indeed, the Sanders campaign has the enthusiastic support of just such a movement—a movement that is notably young and diverse.[333] A recent update from Iowa[334] even revealed that the campaign has had about 44,000 volunteers in that state alone, and, more broadly, has received a record-breaking five million individual donations from about 1.3 million Americans. But why is a "political revolution" coalescing around this specific old white guy?

In short, Bernie Sanders has an inspiring political vision that is firmly grounded in the material conditions of the working class. He has been consistently fighting for our interests for decades,[335] most notably when it was unpopular to do so. This is why Bernie is one of the few trustworthy politicians in recent memory. In addition to his exclusively grassroots campaign finance model, his long career in politics demonstrates beyond a reasonable doubt that he is, in all likelihood, incorruptible. With our help, a Sanders presidency could successfully confront our major enemies; the oligarchic billionaire class and climate change.[336]

Defeating Trump and Beyond

There's another elephant in the room, but this one doesn't belong here. I'm referring to Bernie's "electability." Pundits from the corporate news media will often ponder whether or not Sanders is "electable" in a general election. But if we can eschew our world-renowned collective amnesia for a moment, we'd realize that these are the same folks who told us Hillary Clinton had a "99 percent chance"[337] of winning the 2016 presidential election. To broach this topic, I'd recommend reading Matt Karp and Meagan Day's piece in *Jacobin*, in which they make the compelling case that, not only is Sanders electable, but he's our best shot at defeating Trump. Here's an important excerpt:

> Sanders has been crushing Trump in head-to-head polls for years now, and his lead is especially strong among lower-propensity voters. A recent SurveyUSA poll showed that in a matchup with Trump, Bernie actually runs a few points better than Biden (and much better than Warren) among voters making less than $80,000, and with voters who describe themselves as 'poor' or 'working class.' And those are just people who are already registered. Of the major Democratic candidates, Sanders clearly has the best chance to awaken the sleeping giant of young and working-class nonvoters and bring them into the electorate.[338]

Unless you occasionally find yourself patrolling the streets with a Tiki torch while chanting "blood and soil," you are probably aware that Donald Trump is a complete monster and needs to be defeated. But this election is about much more than ousting an ostensible aberration. A competent historical analysis reveals that Trumpism emerged from specific material conditions. Although the term "economic anxiety" can function as a racist dog whistle, it is also a very real phenomenon.

As we all know now (and should have known all along), Trump is simply an opportunistic con man and a pathological liar. But he *did* tap into a deep-seated and justifiable distrust of the American political establishment, and for that he was awarded the presidency. Bernie Sanders not only has bona fide anti-establishment street cred, but he is committed to replacing neoliberalism with a system that works for the 99 percent. In addition to raising the American standard of living dramatically, this could prevent the rise of another orange-tinted nationalist somewhere down the line.

Picture This

Picture this: Democratic nominee Elizabeth Warren confronts Donald Trump about his endless lies—while she herself has been lying about her ancestry for decades.[339] Picture Warren confronting Trump about his inconsistent rhetoric or his reactionary ideology—when she herself had previously been a registered Republican until 1995.[340] Or picture Pete Buttigieg confronting Trump on racism—after he himself fired South Bend's first Black police chief[341] and after his own campaign lied about support from the Black community.[342]

Picture Joe Biden confronting Trump on racism after he himself supported segregation efforts (not to mention mass incarceration and the racist War on Drugs). Picture him debating Trump on jobs and the economy when he himself supported NAFTA, a trade policy that outsourced hundreds of thousands of American jobs. Picture him debating Trump on foreign policy after he himself voted for the invasion of Iraq and oversaw the destruction of Libya and the drone-bombing of thousands of civilians overseas. Picture him attempting to secure the millennial vote after helping make sure American borrowers can't discharge their student loan debt through bankruptcy.

We've seen that movie already—back in 2016.

Now picture this: An honest, uncorrupted, scandal-free politician with a four-decade record of consistently fighting for average citizens confronting a washed-up Reality TV host and sleazy billionaire who brags about sexual assault and who demonstrates his corruption on a near daily basis. Picture someone who voted against the invasion of Iraq and drafted legislation to end U.S. involvement in Saudi Arabia's genocidal war in Yemen[343] debating a president who drops a bomb every twelve minutes[344] and is attempting to initiate a war with Iran.[345] Picture a progressive Jew whose family members were murdered in the Holocaust[346] deposing a right-wing bigot who concentration camps[347] and whose conspiracy mongering helped the largest act of anti-Semitic terrorism[348] in American history.

Sometimes you just have to fight fire with water.

Lessons in Confronting America's Anti-Cuba Political Dogma

FEBRUARY 25, 2020

The U.S. presidential primaries are not only a time for candidates to be publicly vetted, but also a time for dramatic and disingenuous smears to be lobbed from every direction. The latest effort to discredit the seemingly unstoppable presidential campaign of Bernie Sanders consisted of prominent media pundits clutching their pearls and accusing the senator of "praising Fidel Castro."[349]

At a recent CNN town hall event, a moderator asked Sanders about his *60 Minutes* comments regarding Castro's wildly successful literacy program during the early years of the Cuban Revolution. In short, Bernie Sanders thinks literacy is a good thing (*Gasp!*). The caveat, though, is that Sanders quickly clarified that he has "been extremely consistent and critical of all authoritarian regimes all over the world—including Cuba, including Nicaragua, including Saudi Arabia, including China, including Russia."

Although he is merely advocating European-style social democracy, Sanders was placed in the awkward position of walking a fine line between honesty and orthodox American political dogma regarding global socialist movements. In conventional American discourse, it is a grave sin to make empirical observations regarding the myriad accomplishments of the Cuban Revolution (or any socialist revolution, for that matter). As we have seen, Sanders is guilty as charged. But another aspect of this topic that is highly taboo is a discussion of what came *before* the revolution.

It's unclear what the moderator meant when he used the word "freedom" during this exchange.[350] Was he implying that Cubans were "free" before the revolution? In the years prior to 1959, Cuba was ruled by the right-wing, U.S.-backed Batista dictatorship, which slaughtered tens of thousands and sent dissidents to literal torture dungeons. There was widespread hunger, homelessness, illiteracy, and little access to healthcare. The popular revolution then toppled this puppet regime, ʾought its sadistic criminals to justice, and reversed the aforementioned ditions, vastly increasing the standard of living for average Cubans.

In addition to its domestic successes, Cuba sends thousands of doctors across the globe on healthcare missions in a practice known as medical internationalism. Perhaps most notable are Cuba's delegations throughout Africa, where it leads the fight against Ebola.[351] Also on the international scene, Cuba provided crucial material support to Nelson Mandela's African National Congress in its historic struggle against Apartheid. Mandela, who called the Cuban Revolution "a source of inspiration to all freedom-loving people,"[352] later expressed great gratitude to his friend Fidel Castro.[353]

More recently, Cuba's advances in healthcare and hurricane preparedness have been particularly impressive. During my trip to Havana last summer, I noticed that there were pharmacies and hospitals practically everywhere I looked. The island began implementing a universal healthcare program in the early years of the revolution and its medical advancements are now world-renowned. Cuba has even developed a lung cancer vaccine,[354] ended mother-to-child HIV transmissions,[355] and recently began distributing free HIV prevention medication.[356] Its number of doctors per capita is one of the highest in the world (nine for every 1,000 citizens)[357] and it has surpassed the U.S. in life expectancy.[358]

Speaking of life expectancy, Cubans have a remarkable capacity to survive the fierce hurricanes that regularly ravage the Caribbean. In fact, during the last 17 hurricanes, Cuba only experienced 35 deaths.[359] For the sake of comparison, 44 Americans died during Hurricane Matthew alone.[360] This is no coincidence. As journalist Branko Marcetic explained, "After several particularly deadly twentieth-century hurricanes, the country simply put in place a comprehensive, all-hands-on-deck national program of disaster preparation, evacuation, relief, and recovery that involves virtually every citizen, from the national to the local levels."[361]

All of these feats have been accomplished in spite of one of the most brutal blockades in recent history. As Bernie put it, "Truth is truth."

Why I Won't Vote for Biden or Trump

APRIL 12, 2020

On April 8, Senator Bernie Sanders suspended his 2020 presidential campaign, effectively making former Vice President Joe Biden the presumptive Democratic nominee.[362] While the Sanders campaign has technically ended, the senator has indicated that his name will remain on the ballot in primary states that have yet to vote. This strategy will allow Sanders to continue acquiring delegates to use as leverage at the Democratic Party's convention this summer while shifting his current focus to the federal government's coronavirus response.

The harrowing news was a gut punch to the burgeoning progressive movement, including to yours truly. Being a perpetually "online" millennial, I recall watching videos of the Vermont senator giving fiery speeches on the Senate floor several years before his 2016 presidential run began. This eccentric, white-haired Brooklynite seemed to be an anomaly at the time, comparable only to Dennis Kucinich, Cynthia McKinney, and a handful of other progressive, "anti-establishment" politicians. During the subsequent years, my support for Sanders only intensified as I learned about his decades of public service and his ability to consistently stand on the right side of history and advocate on behalf of struggling, working-class Americans. For every modern social and political issue, there always seemed to be accompanying video footage of Bernie in the '80s or '90s gracefully articulating a refined and firm moral outlook.

In addition to Bernie's impressive résumé of legislative landmarks,[363] this unwavering progressive has also contributed immeasurably to the culture of American politics, expanding our political imagination regarding what is possible. In the last five years, Sanders ran two grassroots presidential campaigns free of corporate influence, inspiring a massive, multi-racial, working-class coalition of small-dollar donors and volunteers. He introduced the voting public to exotic proposals like Medicare for All, student debt forgiveness, tuition-free public college, and raising the minimum wage to a living wage. Because of Bernie's ongoing, people-powered "political revolution," these policy proposals—which are realities in less wealthy countries—have become overwhelmingly popular ideas in the United States. As Nelson Mandela allegedly said,

"It always seems impossible until it's done."

I was fortunate enough to attend a beautiful and inspiring Bernie Sanders rally last February—an event I perceived as a tangible landmark in my own journey as a progressive. But now that Bernie appears to be out of the race, American voters are left with precisely two viable presidential candidates: Joe Biden and Donald Trump. After reading my brief summary of Trump's rise to power (page 65), it should be clear I'd never vote for such a vile creature. Let's have a look at the other guy.

As I've previously detailed,[364] Joe Biden's record is at least as abysmal as Trump's. For instance, during his career as a senator, the Delaware politician supported racial segregation and opposed women's reproductive rights. He said he didn't want his kids to grow up in a "racial jungle"[365] and eulogized infamous racist and personal friend Strom Thurmond.[366] As an architect of the 1994 "crime bill," Biden helped accelerate the mass incarceration of Black and Brown Americans. He utilized the racist rhetoric of the War on Drugs and supported its draconian policies. He played a central role in crafting legislation for the job-killing North American Free Trade Agreement (NAFTA) and the authoritarian PATRIOT Act. He used his influence in the Senate to push the Bush administration's agenda, gaining crucial Democratic support for the invasion of Iraq, which resulted in hundreds of thousands of civilian deaths. His 2005 bankruptcy bill significantly worsened the impact of the 2008 financial crisis and made it impossible for Americans to discharge their student loan debt through bankruptcy. The former vice president has also been accused of unwanted touching by eight women. More recently, a former staffer revealed additional details of a 1993 incident, alleging that Biden "penetrated [her] with his fingers" without her consent.[367]

Regardless of the specifics, many are willing to overlook Biden's "problematic" history. To liberals and conventional Democrats, the singular goal is making Trump a one-term president. What the prospect of a Biden presidency represents to these folks is a "return to normalcy." They miss the Obama years, when Uncle Joe was V.P. and a young, intelligent, articulate, charismatic, and inspiring leader was at the helm. To Black Americans and other minorities, Obama represented a monumental moment in American history, a realization of the civil rights movement, when—*finally*—people of color were represented by the highest office in the land. But, as uncomfortable as it might be, we must examine the unsavory history of the Obama administration. Here are some of the seldom discussed policies and outcomes of Barack Obama's presidency, all of which former Vice President Joe Biden shares responsibility for:

» contributed to the destruction of Black wealth[368]
» deported more immigrants than any other administration[369]
» detained immigrant families in cages (which his administration also built)[370]
» prosecuted more whistleblowers under the Espionage Act than all previous administrations combined[371]
» conducted ten times more drone strikes than his predecessor, killing thousands (about 90 percent of the victims were civilians)[372][373]
» killed three American citizens abroad, including a 16-year-old boy (as part of his assassination program)[374][375]
» helped overthrow the democratically elected government in Honduras and supported the subsequent regime[376]
» Helped overthrow the Ukrainian government in a violent, right-wing coup and supported the subsequent regime (which included neo-Nazis)[377]
» spied on millions of American citizens without their knowledge or consent and expanded domestic surveillance powers mere days before Trump took office[378]
» filed a petition to grant the Bush administration immunity against all civil and criminal charges related to the Iraq War[379]

The U.S.-led NATO intervention in Libya was particularly disastrous.[380] In a disturbingly ironic twist, the actions of America's first Black president contributed to the return of slavery[381] in a nation that previously enjoyed the highest standard of living in all of Africa.[382] In all, the former president's legacy—his crowning achievement—was passing a Heritage Foundation-inspired healthcare plan[383] that left the for-profit system completely intact, failing to even provide a public option. More than a decade after the passage of the Affordable Care Act, tens of thousands of Americans still die every year due to lack of access to healthcare. On Inauguration Day, 2017, the editors of *Jacobin* magazine began their analysis of Obama's tenure with a somber observation:

> Eight years ago, Barack Obama walked into the White House after raising the hopes of a country that an alternative to the brutality of the Bush years, and the desultory character of American politics more broadly, was possible. Those hopes were quickly dashed.[384]

My critique of the Obama administration is not a personal attack against Barack Obama; it is simply meant to illustrate the *optimal results* of a neoliberal political system that is designed to serve the interests of the capitalist class. The harsh realities Sanders often discusses—wealth concentration, widespread poverty, mass incarceration, wars for profit, etc.—continue unabated, regardless of which political party the president belongs to. The Democratic Party and the Republican Party are simply two symbiotic components of what Marx called the "dictatorship of the bourgeoisie." As Antonio Gramsci allegedly said, "The historical unity of the ruling class is realized in the state."[385] By seeking to empower the working class, Sanders (an independent) represented the first imperfect, yet viable departure from this paradigm in my lifetime. To myself and many others on the Left, Bernie *was* our "compromise" candidate.

When publicly revealing our decision to repudiate the two-party system, independent voters like myself are endlessly accused of essentially "ruining the election" in various ways. An overview of these accusations is embodied by the following tweet from author Seth Grahame-Smith:

> "Never Biden" = a vote for Trump
> "I'm voting Green Party" = a vote for Trump
> "Write in Bernie" = a vote for Trump
> "Meh I'll stay home" = a vote for Trump
> If you're a Trump voter, own it. But don't dress it up as a protest.[386]

There you have it, folks. If you vote for the Green Party candidate or write in "Bernie Sanders," the volunteers at your local polling place put down another tally for Donny. If you stay home, they'll figure that out too, and—you guessed it—put another one down for the Orange Menace. Don't think about the math; just feel *very bad*.

But, in all seriousness, this popular notion contains a fallacious implication that needs to be dismantled. For the aforementioned premise to have even a shred of validity, the voter in question would have to, first of all, believe that Biden is "better than Trump." Secondly, the voter would have to be at least *open* to voting for Biden under certain circumstances. I fall into neither of these categories. The immeasurable malevolence of both Biden and Trump is too overwhelming to somehow determine (by what metric?) which candidate is "less evil." It would be like choosing between lethal injection and a firing squad, or between Jeffrey Dahmer and John Wayne Gacy.

Another common election-time trope is the notion that independent voters and nonvoters are somehow "privileged"—embodied by this Mehdi Hasan tweet:

> Just a warning: I have no tolerance for people telling me that they're ok with a 2nd Trump term or that 'they're all the same'. Some of us, especially those of us who are Muslims and immigrants, don't have your privilege. So unfollow me, or prepare to be slammed and/or blocked.[387]

Journalist Sana Saeed responded to Hasan by saying, "The people I see espousing a non-voting perspective are mainly brown, black, immigrant low-income voters; many are people without healthcare, in student debt. It's not always a privilege to exercise the choice to not vote: often it's rooted in manufactured disenfranchisement."[388] Saeed continued by clarifying that "to many working class, immigrant, black, brown, undocumented, [and] Muslim" people, candidates like Biden and Trump are the same.

The sentiments expressed by Sana Saeed are indeed supported by the relevant data. The notion that those who refuse to vote for the candidates offered by the two corporate political parties are "privileged" is refuted by the fact that nonvoters are disproportionately poor and non-white.[389]

Also, white supremacy wasn't crudely devised by Donald Trump in 2016; it is a concept that is deeply ingrained in American history and culture, and has been a horrifying reality for Black and Brown people since this nation's ghastly foundation. After decades of neoliberal decay, this hatred found fertile soil for its Trumpian re-emergence.

Although I am not a member of any marginalized group, I *am* a working class American. My interests are not abstract, but based on my material conditions. I work two jobs and worry on a weekly basis about whether I'll be able to pay rent, go to the doctor, afford groceries, and make my student loan payments. Joe Biden and the Democratic Party more broadly are directly responsible for these conditions I (and others like me) face. True privilege belongs to those who can effortlessly glide through this neoliberal nightmare, unaware of its existence while denouncing those who are struggling to survive it.

Despite the aforementioned vitriol from liberal pundits, there are occasionally slightly more diplomatic Democrats who insist that their candidate can make changes[390] in order to accommodate progressive voters.[391] The first problem with this naiveté is that Biden, whose career was bankrolled by the credit card industry,[392] spent roughly four decades doing the bidding of corporate America. He even told Wall Street donors last year that "nothing would fundamentally change" if he became president.[393]

But the issue that should cast the most doubt on this naïve optimism toward Biden's ability to "change" is his vast history of lying.[394] [395] Joe Biden has lied about teaching at the University of Pennsylvania, about his support for the Iraq War, about his role in silencing Anita Hill, about allegedly being arrested in South Africa, about his ties to the fossil fuel industry, and has lied *extensively* about his involvement in the civil rights movement.[396] Biden's 1988 presidential campaign was even derailed by a plagiarism scandal.[397] How can we trust that this man will reverse a lifetime of conservative policy decisions when we can't even believe a single sentence that falls from his lips?

* * *

Not only would voting for Joe Biden amount to a tacit endorsement of vicious imperialism and the neoliberal austerity that has affected me personally, but it would be an invitation for the U.S. to start this whole process over again; the process that created Trump. Gradually destroy social programs or privatize them, dismantle unions, ship jobs overseas, keep wages flat, let infrastructure deteriorate, spend exorbitant amounts on war, and then, after decades of these attacks on the working class, some faux-populist con man inevitably comes along to blame immigrants and Muslims. Suddenly, the *true* American values—xenophobia, sexism, white supremacy, genocidal colonialism—come bubbling to the surface and a neo-fascist movement is born. As Lenin allegedly said, fascism is just capitalism in decay.

As Bernie Sanders recently proclaimed, "the struggle continues."[398] And the progressive political movement associated with this struggle is entirely incompatible with corporate-funded governance, militarism, neoliberal austerity, and capitalism more broadly. It is incompatible with a predatory economic system that profits from death and suffering by commodifying our basic necessities.

The Democratic Party establishment thought it could defeat an entire political movement by marginalizing a single man. But, as Bernie pointed out constantly, this was never about him in the first place (his campaign slogan was "Not Me, Us"). Democratic elites and their allies in the media thought they could prevail by coalescing behind a cognitively malfunctioning war criminal who openly despises young people[399] and lies on a regular basis. They thought they could use voters as human shields[400] to distract the general public from their crumbling façade and their rotting core. And now they think they can blackmail progressives with tired voter-shaming tactics. Well listen here, Jack—you're barking up the wrong tree.

Barring some unforeseen miracle, the White House will be occupied by a reactionary, racist creep for the next four years. Whether this individual plays for the red team or the blue team is irrelevant; both candidates uphold this sadistic system and both are utterly repulsive human beings. Our movement must look beyond the narrow confines of the American presidency to build working-class power through labor unions, mutual aid, boycotts, community defense, socialist political parties, and other militant solidarity efforts that exist outside the realm of this sham political system. The choice is not between Trump and Biden, but between socialism and barbarism.

Imperialist Propaganda and the New Cold War With China

MAY 8, 2020

> "When war is declared, truth is the first casualty."
> –Arthur Ponsonby

On January 24, a headline in the right-wing *Washington Times* read, "Coronavirus may have originated in a lab linked to China's biowarfare program."[401] The claim was largely debunked and ignored. However, the story was then notably resuscitated by *Washington Post* columnist Josh Rogin in April.[402] By the end of the piece, Rogin admitted, "We don't know whether the novel coronavirus originated in the Wuhan lab." Shortly thereafter, the claim spread to Fox News and other mainstream outlets. Soon enough, Secretary of State Mike Pompeo and President Trump publicly promoted the unfounded conspiracy theory.[403]

According to prominent sources within the scientific community, the virus in question almost certainly has natural origins. For instance, an article featured in the prestigious scientific journal *Nature* explained:

> Our analyses clearly show that SARS-CoV-2 is not a laboratory construct or a purposefully manipulated virus. [...] Instead, we propose two scenarios that can plausibly explain the origin of SARS-CoV-2: (i) natural selection in an animal host before zoonotic transfer; and (ii) natural selection in humans following zoonotic transfer. We also discuss whether selection during passage could have given rise to SARS-CoV-2.[404]

Furthermore, *The Lancet* published a letter signed by 27 public health scientists from eight countries who "strongly condemn conspiracy theories suggesting that COVID-19 does not have a natural origin." The letter continues by clarifying that "scientists from multiple countries have published and analyzed genomes of the causative agent, severe acute respiratory syndrome coronavirus 2 (SARS-CoV-2), and they overwhelmingly conclude that this coronavirus originated in wildlife, as have so many other emerging pathogens."[405]

In short, the sensational claim that the virus originated in a Chinese lab has absolutely no supporting evidence.[406] This specific case of anti-China propaganda is simply fuel on the pre-existing fire of unfounded Western smears[407] against this rising power in the East. For instance, in August of 2018, prominent Western news media outlets began claiming that the United Nations had compiled reports of Chinese government "internment camps" in which as many as one million ethnic Uyghur Muslims were being held. However, upon further inspection, the claim deteriorated. It turned out that the U.N. as a whole had made no such statement, and that the explosive assertion came from a *single individual*, Gay McDougall, who was the sole American member of the independent Committee on the Elimination of Racial Discrimination.[408]

According to the Associated Press, McDougall "did not specify a source for that information in her remarks at the [U.N.] hearing." Despite the complete absence of evidence for this serious charge, more propaganda was subsequently generated by shady Western sources, including a U.S. government-funded "activist group" called the Network of Chinese Human Rights Defenders (CHRD). According to *The Grayzone*, "the board of the organization is a Who's Who of exiled Chinese anti-government activists."[409] The CHRD has even endorsed Chinese dissident Liu Xiaobo, a neoconservative who has expressed racist views toward Chinese people and supports colonialism.[410] A report issued by CHRD arrived at its estimate of one million ethnic Uyghurs being detained by interviewing a total of eight people.

Another prominent source for such allegations against China is a colorful character named Adrian Zenz. Zenz is a German evangelical Christian who has said he is "led by God"[411] in his efforts to confront the Chinese government. Despite his right-wing disposition, dubious research,[412] and lack of academic credentials, Zenz's "reporting" has been featured on myriad mainstream media outlets and even independent, left-leaning programs like *Democracy Now!* Zenz is a senior fellow at the

Victims of Communism Memorial Foundation, a far-right organization that recently blamed communism for global COVID-19 deaths.[413]

During his recent trip to China, journalist Danny Haiphong didn't see "internment camps" in Xinjiang Province. Haiphong further explained that "it is difficult to walk more than a mile without running into a mosque. Every street sign in the city is translated in both Mandarin and Uyghur languages. Security is more plentiful in Ürümqi than in Beijing or Xi'an, and for good reason. Most Westerners are unaware that Xinjiang Province is the site of numerous terror attacks that have taken the lives of hundreds of people."[414] Due to the ongoing threat of Islamist terrorism, Xinjiang "has set up vocational and training centers in accordance with the law to provide courses on Mandarin, laws, vocational skills and deradicalization programs for people influenced by religious extremism and terrorism."[415]

Nevertheless, relying heavily on unsubstantiated Western propaganda[416] of the aforementioned variety, the U.S. House of Representatives passed the Uyghur Human Rights Policy Act late last year.[417] The bill, which includes additional economic sanctions, is part of a larger pattern of new Cold War-style escalations between the two powerful nations. With these tensions comes a surge in Sinophobic hate crimes buttressed by bipartisan,[418] racist rhetoric from American politicians, replacing the hysterical Russophobia[419] of yesteryear. As noted in the *New York Times*, this onslaught is "reminiscent of the kind faced by American Muslims, Arabs and South Asians in the United States after the terrorist attacks of September 11, 2001."[420]

After its astonishingly successful response to the recent coronavirus outbreak,[421] China has found itself further entrenched in a hybrid war with the U.S. empire. As journalist Pepe Escobar explained, "For the first time since the start of Deng Xiaoping's reforms in 1978, Beijing openly regards the U.S. as a threat..."[422] It is certainly true that China is undermining America's global hegemony by engaging in international solidarity efforts[423] with nations that have historically been in the crosshairs of U.S. imperialism (Venezuela, Iran, Cuba, North Korea, etc.). Due to the evident domestic decline of American society, this ongoing cooperation between those consistently demonized, sanctioned, invaded, or otherwise targeted by the West could become a model for a multi-polar global future.[424]

* * *

On October 10, 1990, a shocking testimony was given to the Congressional Human Rights Caucus by a 15-year-old girl named Nayirah. The distraught teenager recounted an event she said she had witnessed as a volunteer at a Kuwaiti hospital after the Iraqi invasion earlier that year. "While I was there I saw the Iraqi soldiers come into the hospital with guns. They took the babies out of the incubators, took the incubators and left the children to die on the cold floor. It was horrifying," the girl proclaimed. Although it was partially used to justify the Gulf War,[425] the story turned out to be false,[426] just like the narrative that was used to justify the subsequent 2003 U.S. invasion of Iraq.[427]

Iraq is not unique in this respect; imperialist lies have also been used to justify U.S. aggression in Libya,[428] Syria,[429] Venezuela,[430] and countless other sovereign nations around the world. Even the justification for the Vietnam War turned out to be fabricated.[431] Such falsehoods have allowed the U.S. empire to violently ravage the globe for decades to protect its economic interests. Now that Socialism with Chinese Characteristics[432] is providing a viable alternative to the battle-scarred neoliberal capitalist model, the imperfect, yet undeniably successful nation that made history by lifting more than 850 million people out of extreme poverty[433] is being maligned with spurious propaganda. Don't believe the hype.

Why Liberals Can't Shame Progressives into Voting for Biden

MAY 27, 2020

As election season continues, outlandish political pronouncements never cease to disappoint. For instance, a Twitter user recently quipped that Democratic presidential candidate Joe Biden could "burn crosses in front of Candace Owen's house and he'd still get my vote."[434] Though unnecessarily shocking, this statement is comparable to remarks that have been made by mainstream voices. In a controversial article in *The Nation*, journalist Katha Pollitt declared, "I would vote for Joe Biden if he boiled babies and ate them."[435] These disturbing sentiments are simply darker versions of a common social media retort utilized by liberals, which is usually some variation of, "I'd vote for a ham sandwich over Trump."

But progressive voters—including former Bernie Sanders supports and other leftists—aren't buying into this deranged hyperbole. In addition to Biden's recent "you ain't Black" gaffe,[436] the former vice president has apparently put a fair amount of effort into making his platform and personal behavior indistinguishable from those of so-called Cheeto Mussolini. For instance, Biden has recently bullied average American workers[437] and voters,[438] clarified his opposition to Medicare for All,[439] expressed support for keeping Israel's American embassy in Jerusalem,[440] and even released a racist, nationalistic, anti-China campaign ad.[441] It's almost as if he's attempting to out-Trump Trump.

The mainstream political narrative is that voters must choose between Joe Biden and Donald Trump. Now that the Democratic establishment has seemingly deterred a progressive insurgency within its party,[442] liberals and conventional Democrats are insisting that progressives overlook Biden's indefensible record and cringeworthy personal behavior due to the "unprecedented" danger Donald Trump apparently poses. They insist that "we" must band together and "vote blue no matter who" in order to defeat this unparalleled threat. Liberals have been using virtually the same line for decades; the current Republican in power (whoever it might be) is uniquely evil. We need to put our differences aside and vote for someone who is slightly, marginally, nominally, somehow less evil in order to defeat him.

The first problem with this line of reasoning is that many progressive voters don't agree with the assumption that Biden is "less evil" than Trump (Biden has certainly been complicit in killing and deporting more people, for instance). Secondly, this approach also ignores the fact that this strategy might not even work, as it failed to in 2000, 2004, and 2016. Thirdly, when voter shaming in favor of "lesser evilism" *does* work, it has the broad effect of conceding to corporate interests and pushing the political spectrum further to the right, severely damaging working families in the process (this phenomenon is often called the "ratchet effect").

This "lesser evilism" is a ubiquitous notion that is proliferated by many prominent institutions in the United States. We're all aware of the role Fox News has played as an unofficial mouthpiece of the Republican Party, but, on the Democratic side, MSNBC[443] is just as hyper-partisan. In recent years, MSNBC has impaired the critical thinking skills of liberals by espousing and promoting McCarthyite conspiracy theories instead of articulating what substantial opposition to Trump might look like. The obvious reason for this behavior is that top members of the Democratic Party—especially Biden—are also guilty of Trump's worst offenses. But these monstrosities are consistently whitewashed or downplayed because looking in the mirror is evidently much more terrifying than a quixotic narrative involving Russian bogeymen.

Liberal elites are using their seemingly endless resources to gaslight progressives by using *their* standards to attempt to shame *us* into voting for a candidate and a party that we're morally and ideologically opposed to. We don't share their standards or even their worldview. They are clinging to the false dichotomy of "red vs. blue"—the notion that the entire political spectrum starts and ends within the confines of our inherently corrupt two-party system. Furthermore, they believe Republicans represent "the right" and Democrats represent "the left"—a pathetic and infantile supposition. This delusional belief also coincides with the logically fallacious assertion that we're "taking votes away from the Democrats" by refusing to vote for their atrocious candidate. Progressives have made it abundantly clear from the beginning that Bernie Sanders, a rare departure from neoliberalism, needed to be the nominee if the Democratic Party wanted our votes.

To break this down even further, we must observe the fact that Joe

Biden is not even *remotely* progressive. Due to his tireless promotion of the invasion of Iraq, his complicity in Obama's murderous foreign policy, and his decades of support for U.S. imperialism, Biden easily has the blood of millions on his hands. However, Trump (whose body count is nowhere near Biden's) has played a significant role in reviving the white nationalist movement, inspiring unconscionable acts of domestic terrorism, including the largest pogrom in American history. While not a white nationalist per se, Biden is definitely an old-school racist (as previously discussed). Biden and Trump have both been accused of sexual assault, and they both lie constantly. Comparisons between Trump and Biden could go on for pages, but, in the end, it must be admitted that it is simply impossible to quantify which candidate is "better" or "worse." It is the sectarian nature of partisan politics that inevitably determines this conclusion for most American voters.

Furthermore, beyond the respective records of these specific politicians, progressives view the two major political parties as being in broad agreement on most policies that are detrimental to the material interests of the poor and working class, both domestically and internationally. Over the last half-century or so, a bipartisan consensus has emerged on issues like endless war, covert meddling in the affairs of sovereign countries (including coups), illegal economic sanctions, domestic surveillance, prosecution of whistleblowers, corporate bailouts, cutting social programs, and austerity more broadly.

To clarify this once and for all, progressives don't see the Democratic Party as automatically "better" than the Republican Party. Both parties are organs of the ruling class, entities designed to protect the interests of capital. To me and others like me, they are virtually the same. And Joe Biden happens to be a perfect poster boy for the two-party system. Whether it was NAFTA, the 2005 bankruptcy bill, the PATRIOT Act, or the repeal of Glass-Steagall, Biden, probably more so than any other modern politician, has had his dirty fingerprints on the legislation that has most profoundly contributed to the decline of the standard of living in the U.S. and the subsequent emergence of Trumpism. Donald Trump's presidency certainly represents a sickness plaguing our society. But we can't treat the symptoms by electing the disease.

Coronavirus and American Exceptionalism

JUNE 27, 2020

America is the Fyre Festival of countries. It is pure hype with little to no positive results. It is a back-alley drug deal culminating in a sweaty palm gripping a wrinkled bag of oregano. It is broken promises, shattered dreams, and shameful regret. All our lives we are told with inflated enthusiasm, with charismatic apologia, that America is a spectacular monument to freedom and democracy, a "shining city upon a hill" and a beacon to lesser nations. We are told our country is "exceptional." And all our lives we wait for supporting evidence to verify these sensational claims as we gawk with confusion at our surroundings.

In a sense, the "exceptionalism" narrative is true, but not in the sense the propagandists and gatekeepers from prominent institutions had intended. As we reevaluate the very notion of American policing—from its origins in southern slave-catching patrols, to its use as a violent deterrent against labor and civil rights struggles, to its ruthless enforcement of Jim Crow and the War on Drugs—we are also faced with a more profound question regarding the very nature of our "great" nation.

America is a political project founded, at first, by the ruthless genocide of its indigenous inhabitants, then, by the colonizing of the blood-drenched land mass and, finally, by the instituting of industrial capitalism through a slavery-based economy. The European colonizers fought resolutely to maintain this barbaric system of kidnapped, forced, torturous, uncompensated labor in what historian Gerald Horne refers to as "the counter-revolution of 1776." The subsequent development of white supremacy as a ubiquitous racial ideology then served the economic elite faithfully as a successful "divide and conquer" mechanism for decades and centuries to come.

As V.I. Lenin's observations regarding imperialism as "the highest stage of capitalism" describe, the U.S. began expanding beyond its own borders—those which were initially forged through violent conquest, land theft, and treaty violations—attempting to quench its thirst for fresh profits. In a stage of neocolonial domination beginning primarily with the Spanish-American War and continuing with covert military coups and death squads in Latin America, Africa, and the Middle East, the U.S. brutally secured natural resources and exploited labor for the benefit of Western capital. The U.S. military, globally perceived as the greatest threat to world peace,[444] has hundreds of bases around the world and has taken the lives of countless civilians. This inherently bellicose institution serves as a de-facto police force for the World Bank and the IMF, punishing any attempt at national sovereignty outside the confines of Western neoliberal capitalism.

The domestic effects of neoliberalism display themselves with such starkness that multi-billion dollar PR industries and corporate news media organizations make it their livelihood to gaslight us and whitewash our own tangible material conditions. As the brief post-war foray into a "prosperous" standard of living was dismantled by bipartisan Reaganomics, disillusioned Americans rejected their own ostensibly enlightened political process by refusing to vote in elections. Wealth concentration continued unabated, with three men now owning more than half the population. The prison population increased unabated and is now the highest in the world. The for-profit healthcare system, claiming tens of thousands of innocent lives each year, continued unabated, and is now an outlier in the so-called "developed world." These are among the grotesque achievements that truly qualify America as "exceptional."

As the federal government doubled down on its commitment to serving the interests of private capital, public institutions and services were systematically gutted. This profound dedication to "profit over people," specifically in the realm of healthcare, set the stage[445] for America's exceptional death toll in the wake of the voracious coronavirus pandemic. The flip side of this carnage is the ability of the ruling class to further enrich itself amidst the chaos.[446] In a natural evolution of what Naomi Klein refers to as "disaster capitalism," we are now well on our way to anointing the world's first trillionaire.[447]

If America was a political satire film, the coronavirus pandemic would be its whimsical climax; its Dr. Strangelove mass-nuking scene juxtaposed with a comforting musical score. Once again, we *are* exceptional, but in a rather insidious and villainous sense. In a black humor sort of way, America is the laughingstock of the world. The Global South must think our chickens are coming home to roost, just as they had on 9/11. Our lofty ideals are effortlessly unraveling before the eyes of billions, culminating in an unsightly mountain of corpses and petroleum-based consumer goods. Indeed, the empire wears no clothes.

As the late comedian George Carlin once said, "It's called the American Dream because you have to be asleep to believe it." In lieu of the fabled "land of the free," what persists is simply an empire in decline—something more resembling an American Nightmare for the vast majority of those affected, both domestically and abroad. All possibilities for revolution or even reform have failed. America is the Titanic of countries; an ostentatious facade naively heading toward utter destruction. The question now is who will survive this final, epic, prolonged plateau; this riveting moment while the glimmering vessel ominously rests vertically, partially above water; this death rattle before rapid descent into oblivion.

Remembering Guaidó's Last Stand

JULY 28, 2020

The year of our Lord 2020 began with President Donald Trump belligerently assassinating Iranian General Qassem Soleimani, who was on a peace mission in Iraq.[448] Unlike many controversial Middle Eastern figures, Soleimani was universally beloved in Iran[449] and played a leading role in the defeat of ISIS in Syria.[450] Shortly thereafter, Chinese officials isolated a novel coronavirus strain after noticing a strange influenza-like ailment afflicting residents in the city of Wuhan weeks earlier. Needless to say, the coronavirus behind what is now referred to as COVID-19 has led to a massive global pandemic. On May 25, with said catastrophe in full effect, a white Minneapolis police officer murdered an unarmed, nonviolent Black man named George Floyd, causing nationwide rebellions and calls to defund (or abolish) the institution of American policing. And that's just the tip of the quickly melting iceberg.

It has certainly been a hell of a year. But there's a special little story that may have barely registered on the radar of all but the most avid connoisseurs of current events. During the first week of May, a ragtag gang of mercenaries launched from Colombia and was swiftly apprehended by Venezuelan forces and socialist fishermen after attempting to invade the neighboring country via the coastal La Guaira State and the peninsula of Chuao.[451] In the wake of this misadventure, news broke that two of the approximately 60 combatants were in fact American citizens and former Green Berets Luke Denman and Airan Berry.[452] This embarrassingly botched mission, coined "Operation Gideon," was quickly revealed to be yet another coup attempt against democratically elected Venezuelan President Nicolás Maduro[453] and the Bolivarian government more broadly. A leaked contract[454] described tactics that included captures, assassinations, drone strikes, and even death squads in order to "liberate" the oil-rich nation.

The lead planner behind the foiled operation was none other than Silvercorp CEO Jordan Goudreau. Gourdreau's Florida-based private security firm was contracted for $212.9 million, yet only offered the aforementioned mercenaries between $50,000 and $100,000 each for their life-threatening services. Silvercorp USA initially began with hopes of converting military veterans into school security personnel—theoretically to protect students from school shooters for a small subscription fee—but the scheme appears to have been shelved.[455] Gourdreau, himself a U.S. Army veteran, teamed up with retired Venezuelan General Cliver Alcala, who had previously been involved in various coup plots, often with assistance from the right-wing Colombian government.[456] This was supposed to be Silvercorp's big break.

As journalist Lucas Koerner summarized, "Jordan Goudreau, 43, was responsible for training a contingent of 300 Venezuelan army deserters in Colombia, who were to penetrate Venezuela in a heavily armed caravan and seize the capital of Caracas within 96 hours." These details and more had been laid out in the aforementioned contract, which, thankfully, also contained an equal opportunity employment clause, promising to be inclusive "across gender, ethnicity, age, disabilities and national origin…"[457]

One of the most notable aspects of the contract, however, is the fact that it named Juan Guaidó as the operation's "Commander in Chief." Guaidó, who initially denied any involvement,[458] is a disgraced Venezuelan politician who clumsily declared himself "interim president" of the Bolivarian republic early last year and has since become embroiled in a corruption scandal.[459]

The political trajectory of Guaidó is fascinating in its own right. In 2007, after graduating from Andrés Bello Catholic University in Caracas, Guaidó moved to Washington, D.C. to study under neoliberal economist Luis Enrique Berrizbeitia at George Washington University. Later that year, he took part in anti-government rallies after the Venezuelan government declined to renew the license of Radio Caracas Televisión (RCTV)—a privately owned station that played a prominent role in the 2002 coup attempt against then-president Hugo Chávez (an event chronicled in a documentary entitled *The Revolution Will Not Be Televised*).[460][461] And thus began Guaidó's tumultuous tenure in the realm of Venezuelan politics.

The young Guaidó continued taking part in anti-government demonstrations with "Generation 2007" youth activists, and, in 2009, helped establish the Popular Will Party with infamous right-wing political figure Leopoldo Lopez. During the subsequent years, Guaidó met with various regime change specialists and wealthy business owners,[462] and even participated in the violent guarimbas in 2014, which aimed to destabilize and ultimately overthrow the government. The emerging political figure then proceeded to publicly whitewash the deadly tactics used by right-wing protesters, presenting himself as a polished and professional advocate for democracy.[463] [464] [465]

Guaidó also participated in Venezuela's National Assembly, spending many years as an alternate deputy, until the 2015 elections when he narrowly secured a seat on the governing body. The opposition-dominated National Assembly eventually selected Guaidó as its president—a position that is awarded on a rotating basis.[466] This new development made Guaidó the perfect candidate for Washington's regime change efforts. Despite still being unknown to 81 percent of Venezuelans, Guaidó declared himself "interim president" on January 22, 2019 with the full support of the Trump administration. What followed was a series of Western media misinformation campaigns,[467] bungled coup attempts, and, after all else failed, a new wave of U.S. economic sanctions that killed an estimated 40,000 Venezuelans in just one year.[468]

After losing his National Assembly seat in early January 2020, Guaidó staged a childish scene in which he attempted to climb over the fence surrounding parliament.[469] The floundering politician then faded from the spotlight until the recent failed incursion. Indeed, Operation Gideon—also referred to as "Stupid Bay of Pigs"[470]—appears to have been a pathetic, last-ditch effort to install Guaidó as Venezuela's president and implement a program of neoliberal "shock therapy,"[471] primarily focused on privatizing the country's vast oil reserves.[472]

* * *

Though appearing exotic on its surface, this quaint anecdote does fit into broader geopolitical developments. Let's first recall that, as part of its long-standing policy of violent imperialism throughout Latin America, the U.S. government supported the aforementioned 2002 coup attempt in Venezuela, hoping to oust popular president Hugo Chávez.[473] However, despite its consistent two-decade commitment to disrupting the progressive Bolivarian Revolution, the world's only remaining empire has evidently failed miserably. This defeated regime change effort mirrors other recent U.S. foreign policy failures, such as that of the devastating Syrian proxy war. In keeping with its increasingly desperate imperial ambitions, the U.S. has now lashed out against China—its main competitor on the global stage and a nation that has aided Venezuela amid the aforementioned brutal sanctions.[474] The epic downfall of Juan Guaidó is not only a tale of personal and professional shortcoming, but could also symbolize a decline in the neoliberal global order more broadly, with new possibilities on the horizon.[475]

The Unavoidable Irony of Mike Pompeo's Holocaust Statement

JULY 29. 2020

On July 29, U.S. Secretary of State Mike Pompeo issued a statement on Twitter that read, "As we mark the 75th anniversary of the end of the Holocaust, [the State Department's] JUST Act Report highlights countries' efforts to provide a measure of justice to Holocaust survivors and their families. We must #NeverForget the unspeakable crimes of the Holocaust."[476]

Condemning the unfathomable horrors of the Nazi Holocaust and empowering its survivors is universally regarded as the morally appropriate stance. On its face, there is nothing controversial about Pompeo's statement. Hitler's regime took racism, nationalism, xenophobia, and other destructive ideologies to their ghastly conclusions; ruthless military conquest, sadistic torture, and genocide. But as morally uncontroversial as the simple act of denouncing the Holocaust appears, we must examine how the *actions* of individuals relate to their rhetoric.

To "never forget" the Holocaust seems to have a deeper meaning than simple remembrance. Is Pompeo suggesting we merely contemplate these horrific crimes on a regular basis in order to prevent ourselves from forgetting the fact that these events took place? This is certainly part of the equation. But another common sentiment related to the Nazi Holocaust (and genocide more broadly) is the phrase "never again." In this context, a crucial aspect of "never forgetting" the monstrous war and genocide that resulted from the poisonous ideology of Nazism is to recognize the foundations and to prevent the seeds from taking root in the future.

Scapegoating immigrants and minorities was a primary tactic Hitler used to justify his atrocities. To begin with, we must acknowledge that Mike Pompeo is a leading political figure in an administration that has attempted to ban adherents of the Muslim religion from entering the United States. Furthermore, the U.S. federal government is an organization that currently operates concentration camps on the U.S./Mexico border, where families are detained in cages without trial, where children are routinely sexually abused,[477] and where the shocking conditions people are subjected to are clear violations of international law.[478] Pompeo's powerful position of authority makes him culpable in these forms of state terror that, as previously detailed, are motivated by xenophobic nationalism.

Secretary Pompeo's boss, President Trump, has recently used Nazi symbolism[479] in a campaign to demonize his perceived political enemies and is currently sending heavily armed federal agents to kidnap civilians and transport them to secret locations in unmarked vehicles.[480] Trump has assassinated a foreign leader and sold weapons to the genocidal Saudi regime to be used against helpless civilians in Yemen, a country that has spiraled into the worst humanitarian crisis in modern times. Throughout his life, Donald J. Trump has engaged in blatant racism—from the racial discrimination at his New York properties[481] to his ad calling for the execution of the (innocent) Central Park Five[482] to his popularization of the racist "Birther" conspiracy theory.[483]

To compare the actions of the Trump administration to the actions of Nazi Germany would thankfully be an exaggeration. But the problem is that a comparable foundation exists. These ideological elements—xenophobia, racism, nationalism, militarism, criminalization of dissent—are all glaringly present in this administration. And these foundational elements are indeed influencing policy. Mike Pompeo is deeply, personally complicit in the gruesome policies that result from these beliefs and is therefore a primary purveyor of profound acts of terror against minorities and other marginalized groups. It is for this reason that Mr. Pompeo's statement on the Nazi Holocaust rings completely hollow.

Professional Oppression and Identity Politics

AUGUST 13, 2020

On August 11, presumptive Democratic presidential nominee Joe Biden announced that he had chosen former presidential candidate and California senator Kamala Harris as his vice-presidential running mate. In a campaign email, Biden proclaimed that Harris "is the best person to help me take this fight to Trump and Mike Pence and then to lead this nation starting in January 2021." In an overview of the news, CNN highlighted Harris's "multi-racial background,"[484] indicating that the Biden campaign's decision may have partially stemmed from a desire to embrace the reinvigorated movement for racial justice in these tumultuous times.

Following the murder of George Floyd on May 25, the nation erupted in protest, demanding justice and accountability. These massive, ongoing, nationwide uprisings are primarily a manifestation of the renewed Black Lives Matter (BLM) movement. As American police departments responded by doubling down on their flagrant brutality, the movement coalesced around efforts to "defund the police." This was encapsulated in a July 6 post on the official BLM website:

> We know that police don't keep us safe—and as long as we continue to pump money into our corrupt criminal justice system at the expense of housing, health, and education investments—we will never be truly safe. That's why we are calling to #DefundPolice and #InvestInCommunities…[485]

On the surface, Biden's V.P. selection may appear to be an olive branch to the BLM movement, as Harris's identity as a Black woman has been given significant attention. This is certainly a noteworthy development in the 2020 election season, as Harris is the first woman of color[486] to run as V.P. on a major party presidential ticket (though others,[487] such as Angela Davis, have run as third party V.P. candidates). Despite the historic nature of this news, we must also observe Harris's troubling decade-long record as a prosecutor in the state of California, a topic that law professor Lara Bazelon summarized in a *New York Times* op-ed. For instance, during her tenure as San Francisco district attorney, Kamala Harris "fought tooth and nail to uphold wrongful convictions" and "championed state legislation under which parents whose children were found to be habitually truant in elementary school could be prosecuted, despite concerns that it would disproportionately affect low-income people of color."[488]

When Harris later became California's attorney general, she fought to continue the death penalty, opposed investigating police shootings, opposed statewide standards for regulating police body cameras, and remained neutral on an initiative that was approved by voters in which certain low-level felonies would be reduced to misdemeanors. When asked by a reporter if she supported marijuana legalization, Harris laughed (marijuana prohibition is a major focus of the disastrous and racist War on Drugs). And this is just the tip of the iceberg.[489] [490] Furthermore, as Briahna Joy Gray observed last year, we should also zoom out from the troubling aspects of Harris's record specifically and contemplate her decision to become a prosecutor in the first place.[491]

Regardless of the extent to which Harris's policies disproportionately harmed people of color and other marginalized populations,[492] her record pales in comparison to that of her running mate. As I previously summarized, Joe Biden's career in U.S. politics has been brimming with both systemic and overt racism for decades. But it wasn't all bad; he did once refer to Barack Obama as "the first mainstream African-American who is articulate and bright and clean."[493]

* * *

In the era of the new Jim Crow, Joe Biden and Kamala Harris have both spent their careers playing the role of the oppressor. The Biden/Harris 2020 ticket proves that the Democratic Party is more interested in engaging in performative identity politics to entrench its corporate-backed power than engaging with the material needs of the American people, especially the most oppressed populations. Joe Biden's disturbing record on racial justice was already a turnoff to many progressive voters and BLM activists. It appears that the Biden campaign sought to patch up those concerns with a quick fix—a damage-control effort not unlike its appeal to women in the wake of renewed sexual misconduct scrutiny.[494]

This isn't to say Kamala Harris hasn't made tremendous accomplishments. Systemic racism and sexism are indeed harsh realities, and women of color truly do face infinitely more barriers to success than individuals from more privileged demographics. But if we place significance on Harris's identity as a woman of color, as we should, it must be even more important to take notice of the identities of those she harmed during her tenure as a prosecutor. After all, in the realm of systemic racism and mass incarceration, prosecutors play a central role in the draconian implementation of state power.

On the ground, this state power is enforced by the police, who have recently come under unprecedented levels of scrutiny. As you know, dear reader, the institution of American policing initially arose from southern "slave patrols" and has subsequently maintained its inextricable link to white supremacy. We are now experiencing historic political momentum as the American people have flooded the streets to demand racial justice and an end to the domestic terrorism of police violence.

Confronted with this urgent demand, the Democratic Party has responded with a stubborn commitment to the status quo. Joe Biden and Kamala Harris have both been intimately complicit in systemic racism, mass incarceration, the War on Drugs, and violent state power more broadly. Given the backgrounds of its candidates, the Democratic Party's plea for Americans to "vote blue" in November takes on a darker meaning, symbolizing whose lives *really* matter in the eyes of our callous political establishment.

Ruth Bader Ginsburg and the Limits of Liberal Feminism

SEPTEMBER 25, 2020

On September 18, Supreme Court Justice Ruth Bader Ginsburg died from complications related to pancreatic cancer.[495] She was 87 years old and was surrounded by loved ones at the time of her death. Thousands attended a vigil outside the Supreme Court building and innumerable additional events took place in her honor throughout the country. Ginsburg was the second woman to serve on the Supreme Court and became known as a feminist icon and a pioneering advocate for women's rights due to her dissenting opinions in cases like *Gonzales v. Carhart*, *Ledbetter v. Goodyear Tire & Rubber Co.*, and *Burwell v. Hobby Lobby Stores*. An email I received from Black Lives Matter Global Network the following day concisely encapsulated public sentiment:

> Last night, we lost a champion in the fight for justice and gender equality: U.S. Supreme Court Justice Ruth Bader Ginsburg. Justice Ginsburg was a giant in the fight for equality and civil rights—she embodied everything that our movement stands for. We stand on the accomplishments of her life's work that have continued to amplify the need to protect and expand equal rights for women and underserved communities. And we celebrate women having a voice in the workforce while also having the ability to make decisions for their own health and wellbeing because of the work of Justice Ginsburg.

In the wake of this national tragedy, Ginsburg's life and legacy took center stage in political discourse and rampant speculation ensued regarding how this event might influence the nation's future.[496] Democratic campaign contributions skyrocketed and Republican leaders began calculating and scheming to fill the vacant court seat.[497] [498] House Speaker Nancy Pelosi announced that Ginsburg would be the first woman to lie in repose at the Supreme Court[499] and New York

Governor Andrew Cuomo announced that the state would erect a statue in her honor. Politicians and pundits memorialized the fallen titan, who had become a cultural icon known fondly by the moniker "Notorious R.B.G.," while others found inspiration in idiosyncratic elements of Ginsburg's persona.[500]

As is the case with other beloved American heroes,[501] the national discourse surrounding the death of Ginsburg included every detail imaginable other than her cumulative record in public service. Unfortunately, the Supreme Court tenure of Ruth Bader Ginsburg encompassed more than just pink pussyhats, rainbows, and "dissent." As with any prominent figure, we must account for the "problematic" aspects of Ginsburg's legacy as well. These include her disparaging statement regarding Colin Kaepernick's racial justice efforts,[502] her positive statement regarding former colleague Brett Kavanaugh (who was credibly accused of rape),[503] her designation of flagrant reactionary Antonin Scalia as her "best buddy,"[504] and her final case on SCOTUS, in which she agreed with the decision to fast-track President Trump's deportations.[505] In terms of Ginsburg's comprehensive legacy on the Supreme Court, the well-known, progressive dissenting opinions are dwarfed by her extensive résumé of anti-indigenous, anti-worker, anti-democratic, pro-corporate, pro-cop, and "tough on crime" decisions. An article[506] in *Current Affairs* highlights some troubling examples:

» In *Bush v. Gore*, "the contentious decision that decided the 2000 presidential election, [...] Ginsburg's draft of her dissent had a footnote alluding to the possible suppression of Black voters in Florida. Justice Scalia purportedly responded to this draft by flying into a rage, telling Ginsburg that she was using 'Al Sharpton tactics.' Ginsburg removed the footnote before it saw the light of day."

» In *Davis v. Ayala*, "Justice Anthony Kennedy wrote a lengthy concurrence condemning solitary confinement. [...] Most notably, Justice Kennedy made no reference to any particularly vulnerable group, instead suggesting that long-term solitary confinement may be unconstitutional for all. Justice Ginsburg did not join the concurrence."

» In *Rumsfeld v. Forum for Academic & Institutional Rights, Inc.*, Ginsburg approved allowing "the government to threaten the withdrawal of funding in order to punish universities that ban discriminatory job recruitment by the military."

» In *Heien v. North Carolina*, "the court held that the police may justifiably pull over cars if they believe they are violating the law even if the police are misunderstanding the law, so long as the mistake was reasonable."

» In *Taylor v. Barkes*, "the court held that the family of a suicidal man who was jailed and then killed himself could not sue the jail for failing to implement anti-suicide measures."

» In *Plumhoff v. Rickard*, "the court held that the family of two men could not sue the police after they had shot and killed them for fleeing a police stop."

» In *Samson v. California*, "the Court decided the issue of whether police could conduct warrantless searches of parolees merely because they were on parole. Instead of joining the liberal dissenters, Ginsburg signed onto Clarence Thomas's majority opinion in favor of the police.

» In *Kansas v. Carr*, "the Kansas Supreme Court had overturned a pair of death sentences, on the grounds that the defendants' Eighth Amendment rights had been violated in the instructions given to the jury. The U.S. Supremes swooped in, informing Kansas that it had made a mistake; nobody's Eighth Amendment rights had been violated, thus the defendants ought to have continued unimpeded along the path toward execution. The Court's decision was 8-1, the lone dissenter being Sonia Sotomayor. Ginsburg put her name on Justice Scalia's majority opinion instead."

I did some digging of my own and discovered additional examples:

» In *Sherrill v. Oneida Indian Nation*, the court ruled against the Oneida Tribe over a dispute regarding its territorial claim. Ginsburg's majority opinion stated, "We hold that the tribe cannot unilaterally revive its ancient sovereignty, in whole or in part, over the parcels at issue." Ginsburg referenced the Eurocentric, racist, and colonialist "Doctrine of Discovery" in her comments.[507] [508]

» In *Salazar v. Ramah Navajo Chapter*, Ginsburg joined the dissent, disagreeing with the ruling that the United States government, when it enters into a contract with a Native American tribe for services, must pay contracts in full, even if Congress has not appropriated enough money to pay all tribal contractors.[509]

» In *Kiowa Tribe v. Manufacturing Technologies*, Ginsburg once again dissented, opposing the ruling, which stated that the Kiowa Tribe was entitled to sovereign immunity from contract lawsuits, whether made on or off reservation, or involving governmental or commercial activities.[510]

» In *Inyo County v. Paiute-Shoshone Indians*, the Bishop Paiute Tribe of California "sought injunctive and declaratory relief to vindicate its status as a sovereign immune from state processes under federal law" and claimed that the state had authorized the seizure of tribal records. Ginsburg joined the majority in dismissing the tribe's complaint.[511]

» In *Alaska v. Native Village of Venetie Tribal Government*, the court unanimously ruled against a tribal council that wanted to collect a tax from non-tribal members who were engaged in business on tribal lands. The Court claimed the land (which was owned by the tribe) was not subject to the tribal tax because it was not part of a Native American reservation.[512]

» In *C & L Enterprises, Inc. v. Citizen Band*, Potawatomi Indian Tribe of Oklahoma, the court concluded that the tribe waived its sovereign immunity when it agreed to a contract that contained an arbitration clause.[513]

» In *Navajo Nation v. United States Forest Service*, the court ruled against the Navajo Nation, who have consistently protested the encroachment of a ski resort on Navajo territory (San Francisco Peaks). In short, the decision upheld the Ninth Circuit Court's ruling that the use of recycled sewage water was not a "substantial burden" on the religious freedom of American Indians.[514]

» In *Integrity Staffing Solutions, Inc. v. Busk*, the court ruled that workers didn't deserve paid compensation for being required to watch theft security screenings.[515]

» In *Chadrin Lee Mullenix v. Beatrice Luna*, Ginsburg sided with the majority opinion which granted immunity to a police officer who unnecessarily shot and killed a suspect.[516]

» *Scott v. Harris* involved a motorist who was paralyzed after a police officer ran his car off the road during a high-speed chase. Ginsburg concurred with the majority that deadly force was justified.[517]

The list goes on. Of course, no one is perfect. Everyone has their flaws. However, when evaluating any prominent or powerful individual, it seems the proper outlook is to weigh the harm inflicted by one's actions against the positive results of one's actions. For instance, Abraham Lincoln's passage of the Emancipation Proclamation helped end the most prominent form of slavery in the U.S. (but not all forms),[518] and because of this, many Americans are willing to forgive his racist views[519] [520] and his mass execution of indigenous people,[521] perceiving his overall contributions positively. By this measure, it is dubious at best to suggest that Ginsburg's full record contains more—simply put—good than bad. That is to say, it seems that her career as a whole caused more harm to vulnerable people than any positive impact her rare instances of dissent may have had.

The simple aforementioned formulation—cumulative good vs. cumulative harm—may be a bit idealistic when compared to the manner in which most citizens evaluate public figures and the process by which these figures are often lionized despite their substantial misdeeds. The cult of personality surrounding Ruth Bader Ginsburg is certainly a notable phenomenon that can be explored in sociological and cultural contexts, but the whitewashing of her record is a crucial aspect of this process that is worth analyzing.

This unfettered, liberal adulation of Ginsburg can stem from a conscious attempt to conceal the unsavory aspects of her record, from plain ignorance, or from a third, more insidious place: acquiescence to the brutality that is "baked into" the American political system and our nation's history more broadly. This is a system founded by white supremacists who enslaved and tortured Africans on stolen, blood-soaked land—a system by and for economic elites. In this sense, Ginsburg's consistently anti-indigenous voting record might be perceived by liberals as a "necessary evil"—a simple extension of the settler-colonial mentality and the vestiges of "Manifest Destiny." The same critique applies to her conservative rulings that harmed immigrants, people of color, and the working class in general.

Beyond Liberal Feminism

It is usually the case that about half of any large population is comprised of women.[522] When speaking of feminism, we often forget that universal issues are also *women's* issues; healthcare, housing, and wages, for instance. Under modern capitalism, exploitation, austerity, oppression, imperialism, and state violence are systemic aspects of daily reality. We must remember that this includes the experiences of women, and to a much greater degree. Why don't we take into account indigenous women, or immigrant women, or women experiencing poverty when discussing Ginsburg's record or government policy more broadly?

Let me be blunt. Recognizing these demographics, is it "feminist" to continue displacing and attacking the sovereignty of native women? Is it "feminist" to rule in favor of employers rather than female employees? Is it "feminist" to deport women back to countries the U.S. destroyed through sanctions and military coups? Just as the lofty, foundational American ideals were designed by and for white, property-owning men, the liberal version of feminism only applies to certain groups of women under certain circumstances. This superficial, elitist brand of feminism is a far cry from a Marxist feminism that seeks a more holistic approach to liberation and empowerment. As Martha E. Gimenez wrote:

> As long as women's oppression and other oppressions occupy the center of feminist theory and politics, while class remains at the margins, feminism will unwittingly contribute to keeping class outside the collective

consciousness and the boundaries of acceptable political discourse. To become a unifying, rather than a divisive, political and ideological force, twenty-first-century Marxist feminism needs to become an overtly working-class women's feminism, in solidarity with the working class as a whole, supporting the struggles of all workers, women and men, and gender-variant people of all races, national origins, citizenship statuses, and so on, thus spearheading the process toward working-class organization and the badly needed return to class in U.S. politics.[523]

American Institutions and Systemic Violence

Deifying political figures like Ginsburg not only whitewashes their crimes against marginalized people—it also further legitimizes a fundamentally elitist, unjust, and undemocratic political system. As political scientist Rob Hunter wrote, "The Supreme Court is a bulwark of reaction. Its brief is to maintain the institutional boundaries drawn by the Constitution, a document conceived out of fear of majoritarian democracy and written by members of a ruling class acting in brazen self-interest."[524]

A sober analysis of Ginsburg's rulings clarifies that America has never strayed from its roots as a genocidal, hyper-capitalist, white supremacist, patriarchal settler-colonial project with economic elites running the government and blue-clad henchmen violently enforcing this agenda through state-sanctioned terror. We are left wondering if the situation has actually improved. Has slavery just been repackaged?[525] What's clear is that the advent of neoliberalism has heightened the perilous and precarious conditions of this crumbling society while technology has allowed strangers to share the visceral horrors that occur therein.

It is time to stop normalizing this barbarism. Performative identity politics and the ubiquitous brand of white, liberal feminism are façades used to conceal the profound violence of American institutions and to paint the "moderate" wing of capital as somehow more humane and enlightened. A society founded on land theft, on commodifying basic human needs, on exploitation, enslavement, and mass murder, is a society that should not be celebrated. And it is a society where the realization of true feminism has—thus far—proven to be out of reach. As Thomas Sankara once said, "The status of women will improve only with the elimination of the system that exploits them."[526]

Fear and Loathing on Election Day 2020

NOVEMBER 4, 2020

Frustration overwhelmed me as I feverishly searched the Uber Eats driver app on my phone, attempting to figure out why I couldn't transfer my recent earnings to my checking account. What was the point of doing these deliveries if I couldn't access the money when I needed it?

The fact that I was struggling financially merely days before the presidential election was an apt microcosm of the dire material conditions in the United States. I knew this election wouldn't result in substantial change to these conditions, regardless of which old, white conservative ended up winning. Beyond my usual observations about bourgeois "democracy" generally being a sham, there was more to worry about this time around.

I was thinking about Trump's cult of goons that would be roaming around the next day, "making America great again" by threatening and intimidating voters.[527] Of course, regardless of their actions, they would be unconditionally exonerated by their devoted faction. The situation seemed more volatile due to the well-documented phenomenon of white supremacists infiltrating law enforcement agencies.[528] To be blunt, it was a strange feeling to wonder if cops were coordinating with right-wing, domestic terrorists on the eve of a presidential election. I wondered how many liberals and leftists were prepared to defend themselves and their communities prior to this ominous occasion. I wondered if it was too late.

* * *

It was election day. Despite my wariness, voting went off without a hitch. I wrote in socialist candidate Gloria La Riva for president and looked through a hand-written list I had compiled to mark the boxes for other local propositions and candidates. Thankfully, there was not a bellicose Trump supporter in sight. As Noam Chomsky recently and annoyingly repeated over and over again during an interview, the process took about ten minutes (this is rare for unprivileged folks). Now it seemed I just had to wait—a process that basically involved scrolling through social media, lounging around, and trying out various methods of "self-care."

The day proceeded as normal. I argued with an "anarcho-capitalist" on Instagram. Giving into my vestigial Halloween-related sweet tooth, I walked to the corner store and spent $7 on candy. My ADHD was bad. All I could seem to do was argue on social media and post seemingly philosophical thoughts like, "Whatever happens today, just remember that reactionaries are paper tigers."

Later that evening, I noticed the progressive Gravel Institute was tweeting things like, "It is an absolute disgrace that it is this close," and, "The Democratic Party is the most incompetent institution imaginable." Things looked bad. But, as I mentioned, things would be bad either way and it is impossible to quantify which outcome might be worse. Both candidates are war criminals, pro-austerity conservatives, imperialists, liars, and both have been accused of sexual assault. Furthermore, both represent the interests of the oligarchy over the poor and working class.

Something that is often overlooked is that both Trump and Biden are "tough on crime" authoritarians. Most people know that Trump has these qualities after witnessing four years of tyranny, including sending militarized police to brutalize and kidnap peaceful protesters.[529] But when we think about Joe Biden, let's remember he didn't just support the 1994 crime bill; he was credited as its main author. Biden has always been a conservative politician. If you look back to the inception of the War on Drugs, it's clear the overarching policy was a form of white backlash in the wake of the civil rights movement's successes.[530] Not only has Biden consistently used the racist dog whistle rhetoric of "tough on crime" conservatism, but he has been a leader in passing the accompanying legislation.

In addition, Biden has called for anarchists to be arrested[531] and suggested cops should shoot people in the legs rather than the chest or head (how progressive).[532] He also wrote a predecessor to the PATRIOT Act and bragged that his crime bill did "everything but hang people for jaywalking."[533] The crime bill also expanded the death penalty to more than 50 additional crimes. And, speaking of militarized police, let's recall the militarized responses to protests in Baltimore, Ferguson, and Standing Rock on Biden's watch as V.P. during the Obama years. Just as foreign civilians can't distinguish between bombs dropped by

Republicans and bombs dropped by Democrats, Americans involved in class struggle and anti-racist activism don't experience less harm when a Democratic administration has its boot on their neck.

There I was at 1:00 p.m. the day after the election, still waiting to see which reactionary, bourgeois politician had won. I thought back to my theory that the Democratic Party was primarily concerned with protecting its class interests by defeating Bernie Sanders in the primaries and was then willing to lose the general election due to the lack of enthusiasm for its horrendous, corporate-backed nominee. After the Rick Snyder endorsement,[534] the aforementioned bullying of voters and "you ain't Black" gaffe, the promise to veto Medicare for All,[535] the clarifications that he would not ban fracking[536] or legalize marijuana,[537] and the tentative plan to appoint Republicans[538] to his administration, I found it extremely difficult to believe Biden and the Democratic Party were trying to defeat Trump. Not to mention they used essentially the same failed strategy from 2016 once again. I wondered if voter shaming and "lesser evilism" would die with the Democratic Party.

I still wanted to know who won the election, while simultaneously realizing it didn't matter. One of the overarching issues people were discussing was the Electoral College. This inherently undemocratic institution[539] is a microcosm of the overall framework of our specific brand of bourgeois "democracy." In the United States, we have other flagrantly anti-democratic institutions like the Senate[540] and the Supreme Court. We also have gerrymandering, privately owned electronic voting machines, corporate Super PACs, superdelegates, racist voter ID laws, and the disenfranchisement of the formerly incarcerated. There is no national holiday on election day, no ranked-choice voting, no automatic voter registration, and the list goes on.

The "land of the free" in no way resembles a democracy. It's no wonder about half of eligible voters stay home. I hoped that progressive Americans would now begin to recognize the intentional failures of the Democratic Party and the built-in mechanisms that exist to entrench elite rule; intrinsic features of the U.S. political system. The desolate material conditions in this "exceptional" nation are an emergency to millions on a daily basis. Given these grim political realities, it is clear that we cannot simply vote our way out of this ongoing catastrophe.

While Heartening, The Chauvin Verdict Is Still an Outlier

APRIL 21, 2021

A pleasant surprise arrived on the annual stoner holiday known simply as 4/20. After a tumultuous year of monumental protests during the deadliest pandemic in recent history, a verdict on the Derek Chauvin case was finally reached. As CNN reported, "Former Minneapolis Police officer Derek Chauvin has been convicted on all charges in the death of George Floyd," and "faces up to 40 years in prison for second-degree murder, up to 25 years for third-degree murder and up to 10 years for second-degree manslaughter."[541] Understandably, celebrations ensued.

But before the dust had settled, we received heart-wrenching news that another Black American had been killed by police. Sixteen-year-old Ma'Khia Bryant was gunned down by an officer in Columbus, Ohio 30 minutes before the Chauvin verdict was delivered.[542] The celebrations seemed to fizzle out shortly after they began. This tragic incident is not only a microcosm of the larger systemic issue of police violence, but a lesson in the naïveté of expecting "justice" from this monstrous system in the first place.

In fact, 64 Americans were killed by police during the trial of Derek Chauvin alone.[543] While attention is hyper-focused on high profile cases like that of George Floyd, is it easy to forget that American police officers kill at least 1,000 people each year—a body count higher than all annual mass shooters combined. This nationwide massacre encompasses an ongoing genocide against Black and Brown people that is consistent with American history more broadly. As many are reluctantly realizing, there is a good chance that this institution cannot be reformed.

While Democratic Party politicians gave disingenuous speeches exploiting the memory of George Floyd,[544] I reflected on the fact that Floyd was killed in a blue state and in a city with a Democratic mayor. I thought about how Democratic president Joe Biden proposed increasing police funding by $300 million[545] and sent the military to Minneapolis to further brutalize and terrorize those who dared to protest this continuous state violence against people of color. This is a systemic issue—not a partisan one. Both parties are complicit. Yet Democrats positioned themselves as the "good guys" and took credit despite upholding the same racist policies as Republicans.

Possibly the worst offender was House speaker Nancy Pelosi, who said that George Floyd "sacrificed" himself for the cause of justice.[546] This was an absurd and disgusting remark—Floyd didn't choose to be murdered. In reality, by convicting him of murder, Derek Chauvin was sacrificed to prop up an unfounded belief in justice within an inherently racist and unjust society. And this belief is indeed an extension of the American exceptionalism that is crucial to the ideological survival of this white supremacist, settler-colonial nation on the brink of collapse.

When anyone, especially an agent of "the law," is filmed conducting a sadistic murder in broad daylight, they should be convicted every single time. The insincere gloating by the political establishment in the wake of the Chauvin verdict reveals precisely how rare anything approaching "justice" is in the United States. We can show this empirically; between 2005 and early 2019, only 35 killer cops were convicted of a crime (a rate of far less than one percent).[547] Based on these statistics and what I previously mentioned about the profoundly corrupt culture of American policing (page 31), it is clear that the vast majority of violent crimes committed by cops go unpunished.

None of this means we shouldn't celebrate the Chauvin verdict. We absolutely should. Seeing the Floyd family's reaction[548] to the news brought tears to my eyes. Although nothing can bring George Floyd back, this outcome is far better than the flagrant dismissal of justice that usually occurs in similar situations. In addition to the prospect of a fraction of justice being served, another heartening aspect of this development is the realization that activism works, that mass movements work, and—as much as the establishment doesn't want to admit it—that property destruction works. Especially under capitalism, where human need is commodified and private property is valued more than life itself, threatening almighty property is one of the only tactics that catches the attention of the ruling class.

We have certainly come a long way. Without the massive protest movement (likely the largest in U.S. history)[549] in the wake of the murder of George Floyd, that violent thug Derek Chauvin would likely still be roaming free in the streets of Minneapolis. While we can recognize the significance of this verdict, we must also recognize that we have a long way to go to organize a multi-racial, working-class movement capable of enacting systemic change. If this is what it took to convict an obvious murderer, imagine what it will take to build the kind of society we want.

Part III

Part III is my conclusion. I like to call it "Lessons for the Left."

This is going to get a little spicy, so, as Samuel L. Jackson once said, hold onto your butts!

Part III

Part III is my conclusion. I like to call it "Lessons for the Left."

With the advent of Bernie Sanders and the prospects for social democracy in the United States, I found myself initially inspired, but ultimately disappointed and frustrated. My political views evolved significantly over the course of the tumultuous four-year period detailed herein. But it wasn't all at once, like some political epiphany. There was considerable overlap between my espousal of Marxism and my naïve hope in a Sanders-led push toward social democracy (you can spot the hints if you read carefully). I believe my political trajectory is far from unique and I believe others can change their minds, just as I did. After all, there is a vast cohort of disgruntled American progressives who watched their dreams of a "democratic socialist" presidential administration dashed before their eyes by a relentless, neoliberal, ruling-class institution; the Democratic Party.

Marxism is both a guide to action, as Engels said,[550] and a scientific lens with which we can view society and analyze its nature. Lenin distilled Marxism into three overarching components: the philosophy of materialism, the informed critique of capitalist economics, and the centrality of class struggle.[551] Historically speaking, it is impossible to overstate the importance of Marxism. In this book, I briefly mentioned a few of the monumental achievements of Marxist governments, including China lifting 850 million people out of extreme poverty (page 101) and Cuba's world-renowned healthcare system (page 92). In his book *Red Star over the Third World*, Vijay Prashad elucidated the Bolshevik Revolution of 1917, the subsequent rise of the world's first socialist state, and the profound inspiration these events had on revolutionary movements throughout the world (particularly in the Global South). The immeasurable significance of Marxism has not yet faded.

The goal, simply put, is for the working class to gain control of the political system and the economy so that industrial production can be harnessed primarily for human need and public good. Once the "means of production" are decidedly seized and bourgeois opposition is sufficiently defeated, universal human flourishing can be persistently pursued. The long-term aspiration of this initial socialist stage is a stateless, classless, moneyless society we refer to as communism. Under our current capitalist system, basic necessities like housing, healthcare, food, and education are largely commodified. Assuming adequate resources exist, Marxists like myself believe these services should be human rights. Building class consciousness, political education, a militant labor movement, and socialist/communist political parties are some of the major projects that await us. But a considerable barrier to many of these prerequisites is a ubiquitous and insidious Western phenomenon: left anti-communism. As political scientist Michael Parenti wrote in his 1997 book *Blackshirts and Reds*:[552]

> In the United States, for over a hundred years, the ruling interests tirelessly propagated anticommunism among the populace, until it became more like a religious orthodoxy than a political analysis. During the cold war, the anticommunist ideological framework could transform

any data about existing communist societies into hostile evidence. (Parenti, 1997, p. 41)

Some leftists and others fall back on the old stereotype of power-hungry Reds who pursue power for power's sake without regard for actual social goals. If true, one wonders why, in country after country, these Reds side with the poor and powerless often at great risk and sacrifice to themselves, rather than reaping the rewards that come with serving the well-placed.

For decades, many left-leaning writers and speakers in the United States have felt obliged to establish their credibility by indulging in anticommunist and anti-Soviet genuflection, seemingly unable to give a talk or write an article or book review on whatever political subject without injecting some anti-Red sideswipe. (Parenti, 1997, p. 43)

Bernie Sanders[553] and many other prominent American progressives[554] have an unsavory track record of engaging in left anti-communism. This unfortunate tendency is extremely detrimental to the prospects for socialism because it essentially disregards the vast accomplishments of previous socialist and communist movements, leaving those who desire progressive change with a blank slate, free of historical lessons or guidance. Whether or not Sanders and others personally believe all of their public statements regarding Actually Existing Socialism (AES) is another issue altogether. Either way, we can observe that a common political calculation is to whole-heartedly embrace anti-communist rhetoric. After all, most of the U.S. political landscape is still saturated with evidence-free stereotypes of Marxism and AES. Given this situation, it may very well be political suicide to speak honestly and accurately about the history of revolutionary movements. But we should have learned by now not to put our faith in politicians.

An important theme in this discourse, as it relates to the United States, is the progressive push for Medicare for All, tuition-free public college, housing reform, and other policies that would benefit millions who are struggling. These and similar initiatives are consistently implemented by socialist countries, as they are in the material interests of the working class. Of course, this is yet another element of Western anti-communism; the whitewashing and omitting of the actual, tangible accomplishments of socialism. It is important to explore this topic in general, but also to point out the inherently white supremacist, colonialist, and often Orientalist nature of such omissions, as they discount and marginalize the important contributions of the anti-colonial and socialist movements of the Global South while engaging in crude caricatures and meaningless accusations of "authoritarianism." This phenomenon can especially be witnessed when American progressives share information about how all other "industrialized" nations have some form of universal healthcare, yet they consistently fail to mention China, Vietnam, the DPRK, Cuba, Venezuela, the former Soviet Union, etc.

Speaking of Venezuela, there should also be a discussion of this chronically misunderstood Bolivarian republic as a modern example of Actually Existing Democratic Socialism. Though social democracy and democratic socialism are often used interchangeably, the main distinction (in my view) is that countries like Venezuela, Nicaragua, and Bolivia have had *actual socialist political parties* elected to power democratically, and these governments were then able to undertake significant progressive projects to benefit and empower the most marginalized among them. But there are still inherent challenges in such a path. Taking Venezuela as an example again, some such challenges include the continued existence of far-right political parties and their violent sabotage in coordination with the still-existing bourgeoisie, large companies hoarding food,[555] right-wing protesters burning food,[556] and ongoing fascist violence—phenomena that are rare in countries that have taken a more Marxist-Leninist approach.

We return, once again, to the realization that the aforementioned progressive social programs have already been successfully enacted by both revolutionary and democratic socialist governments around the world—not just by Western bourgeois welfare states (or "social democracies"). We therefore have numerous historical models regarding how to accomplish these transformations outside of the false notion of socialism that has found its way into U.S. political consciousness (which is essentially just social democracy accompanied by vaguely socialist rhetoric). However we might ultimately build socialism, it won't be through an inherently capitalist and imperialist institution like the Democratic Party. That much should be clear by now (great American socialist Eugene Debs even recognized this in 1912).[557]

Aside from their inherently bourgeois character, another problem with these Western social democracies is how they generate much of their enormous wealth. As is the case with more powerful nations like the United States, Great Britain, and France, the seemingly benevolent Scandinavian countries are also guilty of brutal imperialism, neo-colonial resource extraction, and for-profit human rights abuses in the Global South. As Carlos Cruz explained:

> The 'Nordic Model', as it has come to be known is hardly a system that we should look to for inspiration. No model, system, or structure that depends on the exploitation and domination of others can be ethical. Western nations and their people—if they are to be taken seriously by the rest of the struggling world—must begin to think about developing socialist political and economic structures that are internationalist and crucially, anti-imperialist at their foundations.[558]

* * *

The progressive political movement centered around the two presidential candidacies of Bernie Sanders has certainly had a far-reaching and positive impact. If nothing else, this effort accurately described the increasingly bleak material conditions in the United States, proposed reasonable solutions, and paved the way for socialists and progressives to become involved in politics. Possibly most importantly, it has softened the blow of the "S" word, especially with millennials and zoomers. (Due to the vestiges of Cold War propaganda and McCarthyism, socialism has overwhelmingly been portrayed as some sort of cartoonish "evil" in conventional American discourse.)

Bernie's "political revolution" ultimately failed, in part due to Democratic Party meddling and sabotage. But if it had succeeded, the successes would have likely only been temporary. When social democratic reforms (like the New Deal legislation of the 1930s) are implemented, those gains can be—and usually are—rolled back significantly by the tenacious forces of capital. In short, not only are the reforms themselves compromises with the ruling capitalist class (and therefore watered-down half measures), but they are subject to the whims of these parasitic overlords. For example, decades after an historic struggle involving a militant, largely communist and socialist labor movement that brought us the New Deal reforms, bipartisan neoliberalism gradually reintroduced the precarious conditions and economic crises that inspired this movement in the first place.

Frederick Douglass once said, "Power concedes nothing without a demand." This demand, however, needs to be exerted through power of its own. We must pursue such power if we truly want to see systemic change. The method, according to Marxists like myself, is for the working class to *become* the ruling class in order to permanently implement this vision, using any means necessary to conquer capitalist opposition (as articulated by Engels in his quintessential essay *On Authority*). As Marx wrote in his *Critique of the Gotha Programme*:

> Between capitalist and communist society there lies the period of the revolutionary transformation of the one into the other. Corresponding to this is also a political transition period in which the state can be nothing but *the revolutionary dictatorship of the proletariat*.[559]

* * *

Despite the setbacks experienced by the progressive Left, I find myself optimistic that, when properly introduced to the ideas of Marxism and the true history of socialism, it is often the case that "non-sectarian" progressives and leftists will respond positively and openly. It happened to me, it has happened to many acquaintances, and I am confident it can happen to many others as well. Discovering the absurdities of anti-communist propaganda and learning the rich, global history of socialism can be a very rewarding and liberating process, and those who have a pre-existing distrust of major Western institutions are inherently more receptive to this type of information. The failures of the attempted "progressive insurgency" within the Democratic Party and the subsequent widespread disillusionment should also serve as catalysts for American progressives who are seeking new analyses and visions for a socialist future. The Democratic Party has been called the "graveyard of movements" for good reason. We must learn from these domestic failures and look to the infinitely demonized, yet unequivocally successful global socialist triumphs of history, along with their guiding philosophy of Marxism. To quote Parenti again:

> The anti-Red propagandists uttered nary a word about how revolutionaries in Russia, China, Cuba, Vietnam, Nicaragua, and other countries nationalized the lands held by rich exploitative landlords and initiated mass programs for education, health, housing, and jobs. Not a word about how their efforts advanced the living standards and life chances of hundreds of millions in countries that had long suffered under the yoke of feudal oppression and Western colonial pillage, an improvement in mass well-being never before witnessed in history. (Parenti, 1997, p. 26)

It is time for progressives and working-class Americans of all stripes to unite and chart a path toward socialism and human liberation. We must repudiate all bourgeois narratives and forget everything we have been told about socialism, communism, and Marxism. The elaborate falsehoods we have espoused thus far have only led us to a dead end. We must organize, educate, and harness our collective power as workers. We can end war and police terror, combat climate change, confront white supremacy, enforce indigenous sovereignty, provide healthcare, housing, and education to all, and create an economy based on universal prosperity instead of obscene profits for the few. From the onset of neoliberalism to the preventable mass graves of the coronavirus pandemic, our steady descent into dystopia has been normalized for far too long. The time has come to fight for a better world. As a much more knowledgeable bearded white man once said, "You have nothing to lose but your chains!"

Acknowledgements

I would like to sincerely thank all the friends, comrades, family members, loved ones, professors, casual acquaintances, internet comrades, and internet strangers who have supported my writing over the years by providing encouragement and positive feedback. I would especially like to thank Colin Jenkins of the Hampton Institute for publishing my work online; Trista and Estrella for reading a draft of this manuscript and providing valuable feedback; Breht O'Shea for reading Part III and providing valuable feedback; and a comrade in Philadelphia for designing the beautiful cover and layout.

Online Presence

I maintain a compilation of educational resources for those interested in discovering reliable, independent sources of news and analysis, joining socialist organizations, or learning more about leftist and Marxist viewpoints. It can (as of May 2022) be found at the following URL:

> https://linktr.ee/MatthewJohn

You can also follow me on social media:

> Instagram @matthewthemarxist
> @thisamericanleft
> Twitter @MatthewJohn666

Notes

1. Puzzanghera, Jim. "A Decade after the Financial Crisis, Many Americans Are Still Struggling to Recover." *The Seattle Times*, The Seattle Times Company, 11 Sept. 2018, https://www.seattletimes.com/nation-world/a-decade-after-the-financial-crisis-many-americans-are-still-struggling-to-recover/.
2. Reich, Robert. "Almost 80% of US Workers Live from Paycheck to Paycheck. Here's Why." *The Guardian*, Guardian News and Media, 29 July 2018, https://www.theguardian.com/commentisfree/2018/jul/29/us-economy-workers-paycheck-robert-reich.
3. "Federal Reserve Board Issues Report on the Economic Well-Being of U.S. Households." *Board of Governors of the Federal Reserve System*, https://www.federalreserve.gov/newsevents/pressreleases/other20170519a.htm.
4. Sanders, Bernie. "Bernie Sanders: America Is Drowning in Student Debt. Here's My Plan to End It." *Fortune*, Fortune, 14 Jan. 2020, https://fortune.com/2019/07/09/bernie-sanders-cancel-student-debt/.
5. "Our Organization." *Hampton Institute*, https://www.hamptonthink.org/our-organization-1.
6. Lemon, Jason. "Majority of Gen Z Americans Hold Negative Views of Capitalism: Poll." *Newsweek*, Newsweek, 25 June 2021, https://www.newsweek.com/majority-gen-z-americans-hold-negative-views-capitalism-poll-1604334.
7. Gstalter, Morgan. "7 In 10 Millennials Say They Would Vote for a Socialist: Poll." *TheHill*, The Hill, 28 Oct. 2019, https://thehill.com/homenews/campaign/467684-70-percent-of-millennials-say-theyd-vote-for-a-socialist-poll.
8. Burns, Katelyn. "Trump's 7 Worst Statements on the Coronavirus Outbreak." *Vox*, 13 Mar. 2020, https://www.vox.com/policy-and-politics/2020/3/13/21176535/trumps-worst-statements-coronavirus.
9. Scott, Dylan. "Trump's New Fixation on Using a Racist Name for the Coronavirus Is Dangerous." *Vox*, 18 Mar. 2020, https://www.vox.com/2020/3/18/21185478/coronavirus-usa-trump-chinese-virus.
10. Lopez, German. "Why Trump's Goal to End Social Distancing by Easter Is so Dangerous." *Vox*, 24 Mar. 2020, https://www.vox.com/policy-and-politics/2020/3/24/21193165/coronavirus-trump-press-briefing-social-distancing-experts.
11. Narea, Nicole. "Trump's Policies Are Putting Vulnerable Immigrants at Risk as Coronavirus Spreads." *Vox*, 19 Mar. 2020, https://www.vox.com/2020/3/19/21184081/trump-coronavirus-immigration-enforcement-courts-ice.
12. Beauchamp, Zack. "The Deep Ideological Roots of Trump's Botched Coronavirus Response." *Vox*, 17 Mar. 2020, https://www.vox.com/policy-and-politics/2020/3/17/21176737/coronavirus-covid-19-trump-response-expertise.
13. Beauchamp, Zack. "Trump Is Mishandling Coronavirus the Way Reagan Botched the AIDS Epidemic." *Vox*, 30 Mar. 2020, https://www.vox.com/policy-and-politics/2020/3/30/21196856/coronavirus-covid-19-trump-reagan-hiv-aids.
14. Klein, Naomi. "Coronavirus Capitalism - and How to Beat It." *The Intercept*, 16 Mar. 2020, https://theintercept.com/2020/03/16/coronavirus-capitalism/.
15. Duff, Jasmine. "Covid-19 Proves Workers Are Essential and Capitalists Are a Drain." *Hampton Institute*, 26 Mar. 2020, https://www.hamptonthink.org/read/covid-19-proves-that-workers-are-essential-and-capitalists-are-a-drain?fbclid=IwAR3aXdsYRgSadI8vP_hwCGkJjtlFLzJRTvWyU104DTuhhqJOIJ07kQxrxFY.
16. Nova, Annie. "Why People with Student Debt Are Refusing to Repay It." *CNBC*, 12 Feb. 2020, https://www.cnbc.com/2020/02/12/student-loan-borrowers-announce-a-strike-refusing-to-pay-their-debts.html.
17. Riotta, Chris. "Teenage Boy Whose Death Was Linked to Coronavirus 'Turned Away from Urgent Care for Not Having Insurance'." *The Independent*, Independent Digital News and Media, 27 Mar. 2020, https://www.independent.co.uk/news/world/americas/coronavirus-teenager-death-california-health-insurance-care-emergency-room-covid-19-a9429946.html?fbclid=IwAR2HA1P87jaKClhb7ESwpA1lVF9qUd_ba2_gTpMXi1gwm4wh2GsThwY-ls0.

18. Britton, Jon. "Provisions for Paid Sick and Family Leave Fall Short." *Liberation News*, 27 Mar. 2020, https://www.liberationnews.org/provisions-for-paid-sick-and-family-leave-fall-short/.

19. Oscar, Wilde. "The Soul of Man under Socialism." *Marxists.org*, https://www.marxists.org/reference/archive/wilde-oscar/soul-man/.

20. Bruenig, Matt. "Wealth Inequality Is Higher than Ever." *Jacobin*, 1 Oct. 2017, https://jacobinmag.com/2017/10/wealth-inequality-united-states-federal-reserve.

21. Mishel, Lawrence, and Alyssa Davis. "CEO Pay Has Grown 90 Times Faster than Typical Worker Pay since 1978." *Economic Policy Institute*, 1 July 2015, https://www.epi.org/publication/ceo-pay-has-grown-90-times-faster-than-typical-worker-pay-since-1978/.

22. "Income and Poverty in the United States: 2017." *Census.gov*, 12 Sept. 2018, https://www.census.gov/library/publications/2018/demo/p60-263.html.

23. Buchheit, Paul. "Opinion: Yes, Half of Americans Are in or near Poverty: Here's More Evidence." *Common Dreams*, 16 Oct. 2017, https://www.commondreams.org/views/2017/10/16/yes-half-americans-are-or-near-poverty-heres-more-evidence.

24. Sanders, Katie. "Bernie Sanders Says 99 Percent of 'New' Income Is Going to Top 1 Percent." *Politifact*, 19 Apr. 2015, https://www.politifact.com/factchecks/2015/apr/19/bernie-s/bernie-sanders-says-99-percent-new-income-going-to/.

25. Moorhead, Molly. "Bernie Sanders Says Walmart Heirs Own More Wealth than Bottom 40 Percent of Americans." *Politifact*, 31 July 2012, https://www.politifact.com/factchecks/2012/jul/31/bernie-s/sanders-says-walmart-heirs-own-more-wealth-bottom-/.

26. White, Martha C. "Why Half of America Doesn't Even Live Paycheck to Paycheck." *NBC News*, NBCUniversal News Group, 6 July 2017, https://www.nbcnews.com/business/economy/why-half-america-doesn-t-even-live-paycheck-paycheck-n780276.

27. Jilani, Zaid. "It's Not the Avocado Toast: Federal Reserve Finds Student Debt Reducing Millennial Home Ownership." *The Intercept*, 18 July 2017, https://theintercept.com/2017/07/18/its-not-the-avocado-toast-federal-reserve-finds-student-debt-reducing-millennial-home-ownership/.

28. Main, Douglas. "Climate Change Will Hurt the Poor and Help the Wealthy, Study Says." *Newsweek*, 29 June 2017, https://www.newsweek.com/climate-change-will-hurt-poor-and-help-wealthy-630155.

29. Bruenig, Matt. "The Real Costs of the U.S. Health-Care Mess." *The Atlantic*, Atlantic Media Company, 9 Aug. 2019, https://www.theatlantic.com/ideas/archive/2019/08/best-democratic-health-plan/595657/.

30. Gilens, Martin, and Benjamin I. Page. 2014, *Testing Theories of American Politics: Elites, Interest Groups, and Average Citizens*, https://www.cambridge.org/core/services/aop-cambridge-core/content/view/62327F513959D0A304D4893B382B992B/S1537592714001595a.pdf/testing_theories_of_american_politics_elites_interest_groups_and_average_citizens.pdf. Accessed 7 Jan. 2022.

31. Hendricks, Obery M. "The Uncompromising Anti-Capitalism of Martin Luther King Jr." *HuffPost*, HuffPost, 22 Mar. 2014, https://www.huffpost.com/entry/the-uncompromising-anti-capitalism-of-martin-luther-king-jr_b_4629609.

32. Kristof, Nicholas. "When Whites Just Don't Get It." *The New York Times*, The New York Times, 30 Aug. 2014, https://www.nytimes.com/2014/08/31/opinion/sunday/nicholas-kristof-after-ferguson-race-deserves-more-attention-not-less.html.

33. "Demographic Trends and Economic Well-Being." *Pew Research Center's Social & Demographic Trends Project*, Pew Research Center, 27 June 2016, https://www.pewresearch.org/social-trends/2016/06/27/1-demographic-trends-and-economic-well-being/.

34. Pager, Devah, et al. "Discrimination in a Low-Wage Labor Market: A Field Experiment." *American Sociological Review*, U.S. National Library of Medicine, 1 Oct. 2009, https://www.ncbi.nlm.nih.gov/pmc/articles/PMC2915472/.

35. "Demographic Trends and Economic Well-Being." *Pew Research Center's Social & Demographic Trends Project*, Pew Research Center, 27 June 2016, https://www.pewresearch.org/social-trends/2016/06/27/1-demographic-trends-and-economic-well-being/.

36. Sagara, Eric, et al. "Deadly Force, in Black and White." *ProPublica*, 10 Oct. 2014, https://www.propublica.org/article/deadly-force-in-black-and-white.

37. "Historian Says Don't 'Sanitize' How Our Government Created Ghettos." *NPR*, NPR,

14 May 2015, https://www.npr.org/2015/05/14/406699264/historian-says-dont-sanitize-how-our-government-created-the-ghettos.

38. O'Connor, Lydia, and Daniel Marans. "Here Are 16 Examples of Donald Trump Being Racist." *HuffPost*, HuffPost, 17 Feb. 2017, https://www.huffpost.com/entry/president-donald-trump-racist-examples_n_584f2ccae4b0bd9c3dfe5566.

39. Detrow, Scott. "KKK Paper Endorses Trump; Campaign Calls Outlet 'Repulsive.'" *NPR*, NPR, 2 Nov. 2016, https://www.npr.org/2016/11/02/500352353/kkk-paper-endorses-trump-campaign-calls-outlet-repulsive.

40. Sean McElwee, Jason McDaniel. "Fear of Diversity Made People More Likely to Vote Trump." *The Nation*, 13 July 2017, https://www.thenation.com/article/archive/fear-of-diversity-made-people-more-likely-to-vote-trump/.

41. McLeod, Nia Simone. "Stokely Carmichael Quotes on Society, Race, and More." *Everyday Power*, 18 June 2021, https://everydaypower.com/stokely-carmichael-quotes/.

42. "How 'Communism' Brought Racial Equality to the South." *NPR*, NPR, 16 Feb. 2010, https://www.npr.org/templates/story/story.php?storyId=123771194.

43. "The Secret History of How Cuba Helped End Apartheid in South Africa." *Democracy Now!*, 11 Dec. 2013, https://www.democracynow.org/2013/12/11/the_secret_history_of_how_cuba.

44. *Democratic Socialists of America (DSA)*, https://www.dsausa.org/. Accessed 8 Jan. 2022. Membership figure updated since the date this piece was originally written.

45. "Where We Stand: Building the next Left." *Democratic Socialists of America (DSA)*, 27 Dec. 2012, https://www.dsausa.org/strategy/where_we_stand/#dc.

46. West, Cornel. "Obama Has Failed Victims of Racism and Police Brutality." *The Guardian*, Guardian News and Media, 14 July 2016, https://www.theguardian.com/commentisfree/2016/jul/14/barack-obama-us-racism-police-brutality-failed-victims.

47. Watt, Cecilia Saixue. "Redneck Revolt: The Armed Leftwing Group That Wants to Stamp out Fascism." *The Guardian*, Guardian News and Media, 11 July 2017, https://www.theguardian.com/us-news/2017/jul/11/redneck-revolt-guns-anti-racism-fascism-far-left.

48. Honey, Michael K. "Martin Luther King's Forgotten Legacy? His Fight for Economic Justice." *The Guardian*, Guardian News and Media, 3 Apr. 2018, https://www.theguardian.com/commentisfree/2018/apr/03/martin-luther-king-50th-anniversary-.

49. Hendricks, Obery M. "The Uncompromising Anti-Capitalism of Martin Luther King Jr." *HuffPost*, 22 Mar. 2014, https://www.huffpost.com/entry/the-uncompromising-anti-capitalism-of-martin-luther-king-jr_b_4629609.

50. Ransom, Diana. "Remembering Martin Luther King and His War on Inequality." *Inc.*, 20 Jan. 2014, https://www.inc.com/diana-ransom/remembering-martin-luther-king-and-his-war-on-inequality.html.

51. "Martin Luther King, Jr.. Quotes & Speeches." *The American Writers Museum*, 18 Jan. 2021, https://americanwritersmuseum.org/martin-luther-king-jr-quotes-and-speeches/.

52. King, Martin Luther. "To Coretta Scott." *The Martin Luther King, Jr., Research and Education Institute*, https://kinginstitute.stanford.edu/king-papers/documents/coretta-scott.

53. King, Martin Luther. "Beyond Vietnam." *The Martin Luther King, Jr., Research and Education Institute*, 22 Sept. 2021, https://kinginstitute.stanford.edu/encyclopedia/beyond-vietnam.

54. Sugrue, Thomas J. "Restoring King." *Jacobin*, 18 Jan. 2016, https://www.jacobinmag.com/2016/01/restoring-king.

55. Jilani, Zaid. "Martin Luther King Jr.. Spent the Last Year of His Life Detested by the Liberal Establishment." *The Intercept*, 15 Jan. 2018, https://theintercept.com/2018/01/15/martin-luther-king-jr-mlk-day-2018/.

56. Jilani, Zaid. "What the 'Santa Clausification' of Martin Luther King Jr.. Leaves Out." *The Intercept*, 16 Jan. 2017, https://theintercept.com/2017/01/16/what-the-santa-clausification-of-martin-luther-king-jr-leaves-out/.

57. "The Story of King's 'beyond Vietnam' Speech." *NPR*, 30 Mar. 2010, https://www.npr.org/templates/story/story.php?storyId=125355148.

58. "King's Home Bombed." *The Martin Luther King, Jr., Research and Education Institute*, 5 Apr. 2018, https://kinginstitute.stanford.edu/encyclopedia/kings-home-bombed.

59. Winkler, Adam. "The Secret History of Guns." *The Atlantic*, Atlantic Media Company,

6 Oct. 2017, https://www.theatlantic.com/magazine/archive/2011/09/the-secret-history-of-guns/308608/.

60. Cobb, Charles E. "Guns Have Always Been Vital to Black Political Struggle." *In These Times*, 1 Mar. 2018, https://inthesetimes.com/article/gun-control-black-self-defense-slave-revolts-nonviolent.

61. "The FBI vs. Martin Luther King: Inside J. Edgar Hoover's 'Suicide Letter' to Civil Rights Leader." *YouTube*, Democracy Now!, 18 Nov. 2014, https://youtu.be/pe5il37e7lU.

62. Jones, Brian. "Martin Luther King's Revolution." *Jacobin*, 4 Apr. 2017, https://www.jacobinmag.com/2017/04/martin-luther-king-vietnam-war-lyndon-johnson-militarism-capitalism/.

63. Christensen, Jen. "Scholar: FBI Wiretaps Show MLK's Selflessness." *CNN*, Cable News Network, https://edition.cnn.com/2008/US/03/20/mlk.fbi.conspiracy/index.html.

64. See note 55.

65. Gage, Beverly. "What an Uncensored Letter to M.L.K. Reveals." *The New York Times*, 11 Nov. 2014, https://www.nytimes.com/2014/11/16/magazine/what-an-uncensored-letter-to-mlk-reveals.html.

66. Prokop, Andrew. "Read the Letter the FBI Sent MLK to Try to Convince Him to Kill Himself." *Vox*, 12 Nov. 2014, https://www.vox.com/xpress/2014/11/12/7204453/martin-luther-king-fbi-letter.

67. Yellin, Emily. "Memphis Jury Sees Conspiracy in Martin Luther King's Killing." *The New York Times*, 9 Dec. 1999, https://www.nytimes.com/1999/12/09/us/memphis-jury-sees-conspiracy-in-martin-luther-king-s-killing.html.

68. Rubin, Molly. "Who Killed Mlk? His Family Says the Wrong Man Went to Prison." *Quartz*, 3 Apr. 2018, https://qz.com/1243402/who-killed-martin-luther-king-jr-revisiting-his-assassination-on-the-50th-anniversary/.

69. Judge, Monique. "Fred Hampton's Death Is Just One Example of the Government's Covert Disruption of Black Lives." *The Root*, 4 Dec. 2018, https://www.theroot.com/fred-hampton-is-just-one-example-of-the-states-history-1830865895.

70. See note 54.

71. Hartman, Andrew. "Martin Luther King and Colorblind Conservatism." *Society for US Intellectual History*, 27 Aug. 2013, https://s-usih.org/2013/08/martin-luther-king-and-colorblind-conservatism/.

72. Scahill, Jeremy. "The Sanitizing of Martin Luther King and Rosa Parks." *The Intercept*, 8 Oct. 2017, https://theintercept.com/2017/10/08/the-sanitizing-of-martin-luther-king-and-rosa-parks/.

73. Gong, Zhu S. "'I Can't Breathe': Minneapolis Protesters vs. Racist Police Killing." *Liberation News*, 27 May 2020, https://www.liberationnews.org/i-cant-breathe-minneapolis-protesters-vs-racist-police-killing/.

74. Ellis, Nicquel Terry [@NTerryEllis]. "Breaking: Independent Autopsy Finds That George Floyd's Death 'Was Homicide Caused by Asphyxia Due to Neck and Back Compression That Led to a Lack of Blood Flow to the Brain.'" *Twitter*, 1 June 2020, https://twitter.com/NTerryEllis/status/1267530485691035664?s=20&t=UunrTVJ5-icwyuBJoVtgug.

75. Burke, Timothy [@bubbaprog]. "Salt Lake City Cops Shove down an Elderly Man with a Cane for the Crime of Standing along the Street: Pic. twitter.com/Pclkhqqtjg." *Twitter*, 31 May 2020, https://twitter.com/bubbaprog/status/1266908354821206016?s=20&t=NBwwQBJORCcOwE2A4YSe0Q.

76. Dessem, Matthew. "Police Erupt in Violence Nationwide." *Slate*, 31 May 2020, https://slate.com/news-and-politics/2020/05/george-floyd-protests-police-violence.html?fbclid=IwAR2_A7nIOBxu7fJojyPVWxMBWuFZ_0p4GrF6KI_7miMsDL1gkH4hOefdpAU.

77. "The Police Are Not Required to Protect You." *Barnes Law*, 26 June 2016, https://www.barneslawllp.com/blog/police-not-required-protect.

78. Sexton, Joe. "New York Police Often Lie under Oath, Report Says." *The New York Times*, 22 Apr. 1994, https://www.nytimes.com/1994/04/22/us/new-york-police-often-lie-under-oath-report-says.html.

79. Holloway, Kali. "Lying Is a Fundamental Part of American Police Culture." *Truthout*, 3 Apr. 2018, https://truthout.org/articles/lying-is-a-fundamental-part-of-american-police-

culture/.

80. Schwartz, Drew. "Baltimore Cops Carried Toy Guns to Plant on People They Shot, Trial Reveals." *VICE*, 31 Jan. 2018, https://www.vice.com/en/article/8xvzwp/baltimore-cops-carried-toy-guns-to-plant-on-people-they-shot-trial-reveals-vgtrn.

81. Goldstein, Joseph. "'Testilying' by Police: A Stubborn Problem." *The New York Times*, 18 Mar. 2018, https://www.nytimes.com/2018/03/18/nyregion/testilying-police-perjury-new-york.html.

82. Friedersdorf, Conor. "Police Have a Much Bigger Domestic-Abuse Problem than the NFL Does." *The Atlantic*, Atlantic Media Company, 19 Oct. 2014, https://www.theatlantic.com/national/archive/2014/09/police-officers-who-hit-their-wives-or-girlfriends/380329/.

83. Cohen, Sarah, et al. "Departments Slow to Police Their Own Abusers." *New York Times*, 23 Nov. 2013, https://www.nytimes.com/projects/2013/police-domestic-abuse/index.html.

84. These observations were summarized from information available on the website womenandpolicing.com.

85. See note 82.

86. Statista Research Department. "Mass Shooting Victims in the United States by Fatalities and Injuries 1982-2022." *Statista*, 28 Feb. 2022, https://www.statista.com/statistics/811504/mass-shooting-victims-in-the-united-states-by-fatalities-and-injuries/.

87. Lopez, German. "There's No Good Official Data on How Many People Police Kill Each Year." *Vox*, 14 Nov. 2018, https://www.vox.com/identities/2016/8/13/17938206/police-shooting-killing-data.

88. "Mapping Police Violence." *Mapping Police Violence*, https://mappingpoliceviolence.org/.

89. Lopez, German. "American Police Shoot and Kill Far More People than Their Peers in Other Countries." *Vox*, 14 Nov. 2018, https://www.vox.com/identities/2016/8/13/17938170/us-police-shootings-gun-violence-homicides.

90. "List of Killings by Law Enforcement Officers by Country." *Wikipedia*, Wikimedia Foundation, 2 Feb. 2022, https://en.wikipedia.org/wiki/List_of_killings_by_law_enforcement_officers_by_country.

91. Haddad, Mohammed. "Mapping US Police Killings of Black Americans." *Al Jazeera*, 31 May 2020, https://www.aljazeera.com/news/2020/5/31/mapping-us-police-killings-of-black-americans.

92. Ross, Janell. "Police Officers Convicted for Fatal Shootings Are the Exception, Not the Rule." *NBCNews.com*, NBCUniversal News Group, 13 Mar. 2019, https://www.nbcnews.com/news/nbcblk/police-officers-convicted-fatal-shootings-are-exception-not-rule-n982741.

93. Levin, Sam. "Killed by Police, Then Vilified: How America's Prosecutors Blame Victims." *The Guardian*, Guardian News and Media, 21 Mar. 2019, https://www.theguardian.com/us-news/2019/mar/20/us-police-killings-district-attorney-prosecutor-reports.

94. Vitale, Alex S. *The End of Policing*. Verso, 2021.

95. When I originally published this piece, the number listed in this source was 89. It was updated to 123 in January 2022. Source: "123 Black Men and Boys Killed by Police." *NewsOne*, 6 Jan. 2022, https://newsone.com/playlist/black-men-boys-who-were-killed-by-police/.

96. Hassett-Walker , Connie. "The Racist Roots of American Policing: From Slave Patrols to Traffic Stops." *The Conversation*, 2 June 2020, https://theconversation.com/the-racist-roots-of-american-policing-from-slave-patrols-to-traffic-stops-112816.

97. History.com Editors. "Jim Crow Laws." *History.com*, A&E Television Networks, 28 Feb. 2018, https://www.history.com/topics/early-20th-century-us/jim-crow-laws.

98. Baum, Dan. "Legalize It All." *Harper's Magazine* , 31 Mar. 2016, https://harpers.org/archive/2016/04/legalize-it-all/.

99. Speri, Alice. "The FBI Has Quietly Investigated White Supremacist Infiltration of Law Enforcement." *The Intercept*, 31 Jan. 2017, https://theintercept.com/2017/01/31/the-fbi-has-quietly-investigated-white-supremacist-infiltration-of-law-enforcement/.

100. Additional sources referenced or consulted for this piece include the following:

101. Helfrich, Joel. "Christopher Columbus Is No Hero." *CounterPunch*, 9 Oct. 2017, https://www.counterpunch.org/2017/10/09/christopher-columbus-is-no-hero/.

102. "Federal Holidays: Evolution and Current Practices." *Congressional Research Service*, 1 July 2021, https://sgp.fas.org/crs/misc/R41990.pdf.

103. Miliband, Ralph. "The Coup in Chile." *Jacobin*, 11 Sept. 2016, https://www.jacobinmag.com/2016/09/chile-coup-santiago-allende-social-democracy-september-11-2.

104. "Soldier Confirms Chile Stadium Killings." *BBC News*, BBC, 27 June 2000, http://news.bbc.co.uk/2/hi/americas/807599.stm.

105. Chomsky, Noam. *9-11: Was There an Alternative?* Seven Stories Press, 2011.

106. Johnson, Chalmers. "Blowback." *The Nation*, 29 June 2015, https://www.thenation.com/article/archive/blowback/.

107. Johnson, Chalmers A. *Blowback: The Costs and Consequences of American Empire.* Holt, 2004.

108. Johnson, Chalmers. "Chalmers Johnson on Garrisoning the Planet." *TomDispatch.com*, 17 Aug. 2010, https://tomdispatch.com/chalmers-johnson-on-garrisoning-the-planet/.

109. "Islamic State Was Fueled by 'Epic American Failure in Iraq,' Reporter Says." *NPR*, Fresh Air, 10 Sept. 2014, https://www.npr.org/2014/09/10/347391620/islamic-state-was-fueled-by-epic-american-failure-in-iraq-reporter-says.

110. Ahmed, Akbar Shahid, and Ryan Grim. "For the Record, Yes, George W. Bush Did Help Create Isis." *HuffPost*, 15 May 2015, https://www.huffpost.com/entry/jeb-bush-isis_n_7284558.

111. "Report of the Defense Science Board Task Force on Strategic Communication." *Federation of American Scientists*, Office of the Under Secretary of Defense, 23 Sept. 2004, https://irp.fas.org/agency/dod/dsb/commun.pdf.

112. "Text: President Bush Addresses the Nation." *The Washington Post*, WP Company, 20 Sept. 2001, https://www.washingtonpost.com/wp-srv/nation/specials/attacked/transcripts/bushaddress_092001.html.

113. "Full Text: Bin Laden's 'Letter to America'." *The Guardian*, Guardian News and Media, 24 Nov. 2002, https://www.theguardian.com/world/2002/nov/24/theobserver.

114. Marcetic, Branko. "Why They Hate Us." *Jacobin*, 22 Nov. 2017, https://www.jacobinmag.com/2017/11/korean-war-united-states-nuclear-weapons.

115. "US the Biggest Threat to World Peace in 2013 – Poll." *RT International*, 2 Jan. 2014, https://www.rt.com/news/us-biggest-threat-peace-079/.

116. Shaoul, Jean, and Barry Grey. "US Media's Silent Complicity in Israeli Massacre in Gaza." *World Socialist Web Site*, 2 Apr. 2018, https://www.wsws.org/en/articles/2018/04/02/pers-a02.html.

117. Taibbi, Matt. "Why We Know so Little about the U.s.-Backed War in Yemen." *Rolling Stone*, 27 July 2018, https://www.rollingstone.com/politics/politics-news/yemen-war-united-states-704187/.

118. Greenwald, Glenn. "The Spoils of War: Trump Lavished with Media and Bipartisan Praise for Bombing Syria." *The Intercept*, 7 Apr. 2017, https://theintercept.com/2017/04/07/the-spoils-of-war-trump-lavished-with-media-and-bipartisan-praise-for-bombing-syria/.

119. Chulov, Martin, and Kareem Shaheen. "Syria Chemical Weapons Attack Toll Rises to 70 as Russian Narrative Is Dismissed." *The Guardian*, Guardian News and Media, 5 Apr. 2017, https://www.theguardian.com/world/2017/apr/04/syria-chemical-attack-idlib-province.

120. Stein, Jonathan, and Tim Dickinson. "Lie by Lie: A Timeline of How We Got into Iraq." *Mother Jones*, 20 Dec. 2011, https://www.motherjones.com/politics/2011/12/leadup-iraq-war-timeline/.

121. Hersh, Seymour M. "Whose Sarin?" *London Review of Books*, London Review of Books, 19 Dec. 2013, https://www.lrb.co.uk/the-paper/v35/n24/seymour-m.-hersh/whose-sarin.

122. Boehlert, Written by Eric. "How the Iraq War Still Haunts New York Times." *Media Matters for America*, 1 July 2014, https://www.mediamatters.org/new-york-times/how-iraq-war-still-haunts-new-york-times.

123. Barnard, Anne. "The Grim Logic behind Syria's Chemical Weapons Attack." *The New York Times*, The New York Times, 6 Apr. 2017, https://www.nytimes.com/2017/04/06/world/middleeast/syria-bashar-al-assad-russia-sarin-attack.html?_r=0.

124. Dale, Daniel, and Tanya Talaga. "Donald Trump: The Unauthorized Database of False Things." *Thestar.com*, 5 Nov. 2016, https://www.thestar.com/news/world/

uselection/2016/11/04/donald-trump-the-unauthorized-database-of-false-things.html.

125. "Islamic State Was Fueled by 'Epic American Failure in Iraq,' Reporter Says." *NPR*, NPR, 10 Sept. 2014, https://www.npr.org/2014/09/10/347391620/islamic-state-was-fueled-by-epic-american-failure-in-iraq-reporter-says.

126. "BBC on This Day | 16 | 1988: Thousands Die in Halabja Gas Attack." *BBC News*, BBC, 16 Mar. 1988, http://news.bbc.co.uk/onthisday/hi/dates/stories/march/16/newsid_4304000/4304853.stm.

127. Harris, Shane, and Matthew M. Aid. "Exclusive: CIA Files Prove America Helped Saddam as He Gassed Iran." *Foreign Policy*, 26 Aug. 2013, https://foreignpolicy.com/2013/08/26/exclusive-cia-files-prove-america-helped-saddam-as-he-gassed-iran/.

128. Hersh, Seymour. "U.S. Secretly Gave Aid to Iraq Early in Its War against Iran." *The New York Times*, The New York Times, 26 Jan. 1992, https://www.nytimes.com/1992/01/26/world/us-secretly-gave-aid-to-iraq-early-in-its-war-against-iran.html.

129. Davies, Nicolas J. S. "35 Countries Where the U.S. Has Supported Fascists, Drug Lords and Terrorists." *Alternet*, 4 Mar. 2014, https://www.alternet.org/2014/03/35-countries-where-us-has-supported-fascists-druglords-and-terrorists/.

130. Schwarz, Jon. "Seven Things You Didn't Know the U.S. and Its Allies Did to Iran." *The Intercept*, 7 Apr. 2015, https://theintercept.com/2015/04/07/10-things-didnt-know-weve-done-iran/.

131. Kamali, Saeed, and Richard Norton-Taylor. "Cia Admits Role in 1953 Iranian Coup." *The Guardian*, Guardian News and Media, 19 Aug. 2013, https://www.theguardian.com/world/2013/aug/19/cia-admits-role-1953-iranian-coup.

132. "World Report 2016: Rights Trends in Saudi Arabia." *Human Rights Watch*, 27 Jan. 2016, https://www.hrw.org/world-report/2016/country-chapters/saudi-arabia#.

133. Butt, Yousaf. "How Saudi Wahhabism Is the Fountainhead of Islamist Terrorism." *HuffPost*, HuffPost, 22 Mar. 2015, https://www.huffpost.com/entry/saudi-wahhabism-islam-terrorism_b_6501916.

134. Carden, James. "America's Support for Saudi Arabia's War on Yemen Must End." *The Nation*, 5 Apr. 2017, https://www.thenation.com/article/archive/americas-support-for-saudi-arabias-war-on-yemen-must-end/.

135. 2015, *Body Count: Casualty Figures after 10 Years of the "War on Terror"*, https://www.psr.org/wp-content/uploads/2018/05/body-count.pdf. Accessed 7 Jan. 2022.

136. This was originally two separate pieces that I wrote in August of 2017. I combined them for this book due to comparable subject matter.

137. Porter, Tom. "Who Are the Alt-Right Leaders and Provocateurs Addressing the Charlottesville White Nationalist Rally?" *Newsweek*, Newsweek, 12 Aug. 2017, https://www.newsweek.com/alt-right-leaders-are-addressing-largest-white-nationalist-rally-decades-650096.

138. "James Alex Fields Jr. Identified as Charlottesville Suspect." *The Daily Beast*, The Daily Beast Company, 13 Aug. 2017, https://www.thedailybeast.com/james-alex-fields-jr-idd-as-charlottesville-suspect.

139. While re-reading this, I cringed at my use of the term "democracy" in this context, and my use of the term "totalitarian" in this or any other context (for reasons many of you will recognize). However, as I edited these pieces, one principle I stuck to was preserving the spirit of what I had written. I wanted to improve the quality of each piece while still accurately portraying the views I held at the time. By the end of this book, you, dear reader, will see how far I have come in my political journey.

140. Sitrin, Carly. "Read: President Trump's Remarks Condemning Violence 'on Many Sides' in Charlottesville." *Vox*, 12 Aug. 2017, https://www.vox.com/2017/8/12/16138906/president-trump-remarks-condemning-violence-on-many-sides-charlottesville-rally.

141. Hasan, Mehdi. "The Numbers Don't Lie: White Far-Right Terrorists Pose a Clear Danger to Us All." *The Intercept*, 31 May 2017, https://theintercept.com/2017/05/31/the-numbers-dont-lie-white-far-right-terrorists-pose-a-clear-danger-to-us-all/.

142. Todd, Sarah. "When Donald Trump Refuses to Fault White Supremacists, It's Every American's Job to Call Him Out." *Quartz*, 12 Aug. 2017, https://qz.com/1052580/charlottesville-white-nationalist-rally-donald-trumps-neutral-speech-was-a-moral-failure/.

143. "Hate Map." *Southern Poverty Law Center*, 30 Dec. 2021, https://www.splcenter.org/

hate-map.

144. Lennard, Natasha. "Neo-Nazi Richard Spencer Got Punched-You Can Thank the Black Bloc." *The Nation*, 24 Jan. 2017, https://www.thenation.com/article/archive/if-you-appreciated-seeing-neo-nazi-richard-spencer-get-punched-thank-the-black-bloc/.

145. Popper, Karl. *The Open Society and Its Enemies*. Routledge, 2008.

146. Vysotsky, Stanislav. "Drawing Equivalencies between Fascists and Anti-Fascists Is Not Just Wrong-It's Dangerous." *In These Times*, 15 Aug. 2017, https://inthesetimes.com/article/false-equivalency-white-supremacist-nazis-fascists-antifa-Charlottesville.

147. "Cornel West & Rev. Traci Blackmon: Clergy in Charlottesville Were Trapped by Torch-Wielding Nazis." *Democracy Now!*, 14 Aug. 2017, https://www.democracynow.org/2017/8/14/cornel_west_rev_toni_blackmon_clergy.

148. Balhorn, Loren. "The Lost History of Antifa." *Jacobin*, 8 May 2017, https://www.jacobinmag.com/2017/05/antifascist-movements-hitler-nazis-kpd-spd-germany-cold-war.

149. "Antifa: A Look at the Anti-Fascist Movement Confronting White Supremacists in the Streets." *Democracy Now!*, 16 Aug. 2017, https://www.democracynow.org/2017/8/16/antifa_a_look_at_the_antifascist.

150. Bray, Mark. "Who Are the Antifa?" *The Washington Post*, WP Company, 16 Aug. 2017, https://www.washingtonpost.com/news/made-by-history/wp/2017/08/16/who-are-the-antifa/.

151. Collins, Chuck, and Josh Hoxie. *Billionaire Bonanza 2017 Embargoed*. Institute for Policy Studies, Nov. 2017, https://ips-dc.org/wp-content/uploads/2017/11/BILLIONAIRE-BONANZA-2017-FinalV.pdf.

152. Kampf-Lassin, Miles. "Socialists Just Showed the Democratic Party How to Win across the U.S." *In These Times*, 8 Nov. 2017, https://inthesetimes.com/article/socialists-democrats-larry-krasner-election-2017.

153. Quarshie, Mabinty. "Virginia Elects Second African-American to Statewide Office, First Latinas to State House." *USA Today*, Gannett Satellite Information Network, 8 Nov. 2017, https://www.usatoday.com/story/news/politics/onpolitics/2017/11/07/virginia-elects-second-african-american-statewide-office-first-latinas-state-house/842720001/.

154. Magness, Josh. "Millennials Aren't Satisfied with Capitalism and Might Prefer a Socialist Country, Studies Find." *The Sacramento Bee*, 4 Nov. 2017, https://www.sacbee.com/news/nation-world/national/article182765121.html.

155. Ekins, Emily. "Poll: Americans like Free Markets More than Capitalism and Socialism More than a Govt Managed Economy." *Reason.com*, 12 Feb. 2015, https://reason.com/2015/02/12/poll-americans-like-free-markets-more-th/.

156. Newport, Frank. "Americans' Views of Socialism, Capitalism Are Little Changed." *Gallup.com*, Gallup, 6 May 2016, https://news.gallup.com/poll/191354/americans-views-socialism-capitalism-little-changed.aspx.

157. Blake, Aaron. "More Young People Voted for Bernie Sanders than Trump and Clinton Combined - by a Lot." *The Washington Post*, WP Company, 20 June 2016, https://www.washingtonpost.com/news/the-fix/wp/2016/06/20/more-young-people-voted-for-bernie-sanders-than-trump-and-clinton-combined-by-a-lot/.

158. Marcetic, Branko. "The Secret History of Superdelegates." *In These Times*, 16 May 2016, https://inthesetimes.com/features/superdelegates_bernie_sanders_hillary_clinton.html.

159. Brazile, Donna. "Inside Hillary Clinton's Secret Takeover of the DNC." *POLITICO Magazine*, 2 Nov. 2017, https://www.politico.com/magazine/story/2017/11/02/clinton-brazile-hacks-2016-215774/.

160. Marcetic, Branko. "It's Still Their Party: What the DNC Purge Means for the Democrats' Left Flank." *In These Times*, 23 Oct. 2017, https://inthesetimes.com/article/dnc-purge-ellison-perez-bernie-sanders-left-center.

161. Sanders, Bernie. "How to Fix the Democratic Party." *POLITICO Magazine*, 10 Nov. 2017, https://www.politico.com/magazine/story/2017/11/10/bernie-sanders-how-to-fix-democratic-party-215813/.

162. Buchheit, Paul. "Opinion: Yes, Half of Americans Are in or near Poverty: Here's More Evidence." *Common Dreams*, 16 Oct. 2017, https://www.commondreams.org/views/2017/10/16/yes-half-americans-are-or-near-poverty-heres-more-evidence.

163. Bacon, John. "What Is Temporary Protected Status: Nearly 200,000 Salvadorans May

Be Forced to Leave U.S." *USA Today*, Gannett Satellite Information Network, 12 Jan. 2018, https://www.usatoday.com/story/news/nation-now/2018/01/12/what-temporary-protected-status-nearly-200-000-salvadorans-may-forced-leave-u-s/1027487001/.

164. Walsh, Joan. "Why Donald Trump Said 'Shithole Countries'." *The Nation*, 13 Jan. 2018, https://www.thenation.com/article/archive/why-donald-trump-said-shithole-countries/.

165. Devereaux, Ryan. "Ignoring Violence in El Salvador, Trump Ends Years of Special Protective Status for Immigrants." *The Intercept*, 8 Jan. 2018, https://theintercept.com/2018/01/08/el-salvador-immigration-tps-trump/.

166. Lakhani, Nina. "'We Fear Soldiers More than Gangsters': El Salvador's 'Iron Fist' Policy Turns Deadly." *The Guardian*, Guardian News and Media, 6 Feb. 2017, https://www.theguardian.com/world/2017/feb/06/el-salvador-gangs-police-violence-distrito-italia.

167. Currier, Cora, and Natalie Keyssar. "El Salvador's Youth Are Trapped between Gang Violence and Police Abuse." *The Intercept*, 12 Jan. 2018, https://theintercept.com/2018/01/12/el-salvador-tps-trump-gang-violence/.

168. Stillman, Sarah. "When Deportation Is a Death Sentence." *The New Yorker*, 8 Jan. 2018, https://www.newyorker.com/magazine/2018/01/15/when-deportation-is-a-death-sentence.

169. Goodfriend, Hilary. "The Machinations of Empire." *Jacobin*, 13 Jan. 2018, https://www.jacobinmag.com/2018/01/tps-el-salvador-dhs-immigration-daca.

170. Schwarz, Benjamin. "Dirty Hands." *The Atlantic*, Atlantic Media Company, 4 Feb. 2016, https://amp.theatlantic.com/amp/article/377364/.

171. Emiridge, Julian. "The Forgotten Interventions." *Jacobin*, 12 Jan. 2017, https://www.jacobinmag.com/2017/01/russia-hacks-election-meddling-iran-mossadegh-chile-allende-guatemala-arbenz-coup.

172. Bonner, Raymond. "Time for a US Apology to El Salvador." *The Nation*, 12 Dec. 2016, https://www.thenation.com/article/archive/time-for-a-us-apology-to-el-salvador/.

173. Fernandez, Belen. "Remembering US-Backed State Terror in El Salvador." *Al Jazeera*, 11 Dec. 2021, https://www.aljazeera.com/opinions/2021/12/11/remembering-us-backed-state-terror-in-el-salvador.

174. "Newly Discovered 1964 MLK Speech on Civil Rights, Segregation & Apartheid South Africa." *YouTube*, Democracy Now!, 15 Jan. 2018, https://www.youtube.com/watch?v=1iiFNj3D_K4.

175. United Nations, 1993, *Report of the UN Truth Commission on El Salvador*, http://www.derechos.org/nizkor/salvador/informes/truth.html. Accessed 11 Jan. 2022.

176. "Joint Statement from the Department of Homeland Security and Office of the Director of National Intelligence on Election Security." *Department of Homeland Security*, 7 Oct. 2016, https://www.dhs.gov/news/2016/10/07/joint-statement-department-homeland-security-and-office-director-national.

177. Schwarz, Jon. "Politico Gives CIA's Worst WMD Liar a Platform to SLAM Seymour Hersh." *The Intercept*, 14 May 2015, https://theintercept.com/2015/05/14/politico-gives-cias-worst-wmd-liar-platform-slam-seymour-hersh/.

178. Kaplan, Fred. "James Clapper Lied to Congress about NSA Surveillance. He Should Be Fired." *Slate Magazine*, Slate, 11 June 2013, https://slate.com/news-and-politics/2013/06/fire-dni-james-clapper-he-lied-to-congress-about-nsa-surveillance.html.

179. Ciaramella, CJ. "The Biggest Lies the CIA Told about Its Torture Program." *VICE*, 10 Dec. 2014, https://www.vice.com/en/article/kwp4m3/all-of-the-ways-the-cia-lied-about-its-torture-program.

180. Ciaramella, CJ. "Hypothermia, Broken Limbs, and Rectal Feeding: Details from the CIA Torture Report." *VICE*, 9 Dec. 2014, https://www.vice.com/en/article/mv58m4/hypothermia-broken-limbs-and-rectal-feeding-details-from-the-cia-torture-report-129.

181. Carlson, Michael. "Clair George: CIA Officer Who Was Convicted of Lying to Congress Over." *The Independent*, Independent Digital News and Media, 31 Aug. 2011, https://www.independent.co.uk/news/obituaries/clair-george-cia-officer-who-was-convicted-of-lying-to-congress-over-the-irancontra-affair-2346382.html.

182. "C.I.A. and Former Nazis." *The New York Times*, The New York Times, 19 Nov. 2010, https://www.nytimes.com/2010/11/19/opinion/l19cia.html.

183. History.com editors. "MK-Ultra." *History.com*, A&E Television Networks, 16 June 2017, https://www.history.com/topics/us-government/history-of-mk-ultra.

184. Wheeler, Marcy. "Democrats Embraced a Flawed Dossier-and Gave Republicans an Opening." *POLITICO Magazine*, 1 Feb. 2018, https://www.politico.com/magazine/story/2018/02/01/russia-steele-dossier-democrats-republicans-216921/.

185. Graham, David A. "The New Intelligence Report on Russian Hacking Will Change No One's Mind." *The Atlantic*, Atlantic Media Company, 6 Jan. 2017, https://www.theatlantic.com/politics/archive/2017/01/odni-report-on-russian-hacking/512465/.

186. Greenwald, Glenn. "Washpost Is Richly Rewarded for False News about Russia Threat While Public Is Deceived." *The Intercept*, 4 Jan. 2017, https://theintercept.com/2017/01/04/washpost-is-richly-rewarded-for-false-news-about-russia-threat-while-public-is-deceived/.

187. Stelter, Brian. "CNN Employees Resign after Retracted Article." *CNNMoney*, 27 June 2017, https://money.cnn.com/2017/06/26/media/cnn-announcement-retracted-article/index.html.

188. Greenwald, Glenn. "The U.S. Media Suffered Its Most Humiliating Debacle in Ages and Now Refuses All Transparency over What Happened." *The Intercept*, 9 Dec. 2017, https://theintercept.com/2017/12/09/the-u-s-media-yesterday-suffered-its-most-humiliating-debacle-in-ages-now-refuses-all-transparency-over-what-happened/.

189. Maté, Aaron. "More Media Malpractice in Russiagate." *The Nation*, 19 Jan. 2018, https://www.thenation.com/article/archive/more-media-malpractice-in-russiagate/.

190. Vitkovskaya, Julie, et al. "Who Was Charged in the Mueller Probe, and Why." *The Washington Post*, WP Company, 22 Mar. 2019, https://www.washingtonpost.com/graphics/2017/national/robert-mueller-special-counsel-indictments-timeline/?utm_term=.3b1f365aaf93.

191. "Where's the 'Collusion'?" *YouTube*, The Real News Network, 23 Dec. 2017, https://youtu.be/9Ikf1uZli4g.

192. Maté, Aaron. "MSNBC's Rachel Maddow Sees a 'Russia Connection' Lurking around Every Corner." *The Intercept*, 12 Apr. 2017, https://theintercept.com/2017/04/12/msnbcs-rachel-maddow-sees-a-russia-connection-lurking-around-every-corner/.

193. Maté, Aaron. "Russiagate Is More Fiction than Fact." *The Nation*, 7 Oct. 2017, https://www.thenation.com/article/archive/russiagate-is-more-fiction-than-fact/.

194. Hedges, Chris. "How 'Russiagate' Helped Secure a Dangerous Arms Deal." *Truthdig*, 6 Jan. 2018, https://www.truthdig.com/articles/russiagate-helped-secure-dangerous-arms-deal/.

195. "Roll Call Vote 107th Congress - 2nd Session." *Senate.gov*, https://www.senate.gov/legislative/LIS/roll_call_votes/vote1072/vote_107_2_00237.htm.

196. "Final Vote Results for Roll Call 455." *Office of the Clerk, U.S. House of Representatives*, https://clerk.house.gov/evs/2002/roll455.xml.

197. "Timeline." *Bulletin of the Atomic Scientists*, https://thebulletin.org/doomsday-clock/timeline/.

198. Liptak, Adam, and Michael D. Shear. "Trump's Travel Ban Is Upheld by Supreme Court." *The New York Times*, 26 June 2018, https://www.nytimes.com/2018/06/26/us/politics/supreme-court-trump-travel-ban.html.

199. Edmondson, Catie. "Sonia Sotomayor Delivers Sharp Dissent in Travel Ban Case." *The New York Times*, 26 June 2018, https://www.nytimes.com/2018/06/26/us/sonia-sotomayor-dissent-travel-ban.html.

200. "The Evacuated People: A Quantitative Study (1946)." *Densho Digital Repository*, U.S. Department of the Interior, https://ddr.densho.org/ddr-densho-282-5/.

201. "President Donald J. Trump's Travel Restrictions Defend Our Country." *National Archives and Records Administration*, 27 June 2018, https://trumpwhitehouse.archives.gov/briefings-statements/president-donald-j-trumps-travel-restrictions-defend-country/.

202. "Deconstructed Podcast: The White Supremacy Court Upholds the Muslim Ban." *The Intercept*, 27 June 2018, https://theintercept.com/2018/06/26/the-white-supremacy-court-upholds-the-muslim-ban/.

203. Marcetic, Branko. "Why Is There No 'Saudi-Gate'?" *Jacobin*, 30 Nov. 2017, https://www.jacobinmag.com/2017/11/trump-russia-bush-saudi-arabia.

204. Sanger, David E. "Rebel Arms Flow Is Said to Benefit Jihadists in Syria." *The New York Times*, 15 Oct. 2012, https://www.nytimes.com/2012/10/15/world/middleeast/jihadists-receiving-most-arms-sent-to-syrian-rebels.html.

205. Glazebrook, Dan. "The $1.5 Billion Campaign to Whitewash Genocide in Yemen." *CounterPunch*, 5 Mar. 2018, https://www.counterpunch.org/2018/03/05/the-1-5-billion-campaign-to-whitewash-genocide-in-yemen/.

206. Landler, Mark, et al. "$110 Billion Weapons Sale to Saudis Has Jared Kushner's Personal Touch." *The New York Times*, 19 May 2017, https://www.nytimes.com/2017/05/18/world/middleeast/jared-kushner-saudi-arabia-arms-deal-lockheed.html.

207. Cooper, Helene. "Senate Narrowly Backs Trump Weapons Sale to Saudi Arabia." *The New York Times*, 13 June 2017, https://www.nytimes.com/2017/06/13/world/middleeast/trump-weapons-saudi-arabia.html.

208. Finnegan, Michael, and Noah Bierman. "Trump's Endorsement of Violence Reaches New Level: He May Pay Legal Fees for Assault Suspect." *Los Angeles Times*, 13 Mar. 2016, https://www.latimes.com/politics/la-na-trump-campaign-protests-20160313-story.html.

209. Kamisar, Ben. "Trump: 'Second Amendment People' Could Stop Clinton." *The Hill*, 19 Aug. 2016, https://thehill.com/homenews/campaign/290892-trump-says-second-amendment-folks-could-stop-clinton.

210. "Donald Trump Criticized for Mocking Disabled Reporter." *Snopes*, 28 July 2016, https://www.snopes.com/news/2016/07/28/donald-trump-criticized-for-mocking-disabled-reporter/.

211. Haberman, Maggie, and Richard A. Oppel. "Donald Trump Criticizes Muslim Family of Slain U.S. Soldier, Drawing Ire." *The New York Times*, 30 July 2016, https://www.nytimes.com/2016/07/31/us/politics/donald-trump-khizr-khan-wife-ghazala.html.

212. Griffin, Andrew. "The Background to Donald Trump's Islamophobic Tweets Make Them Even Worse." *The Independent*, Independent Digital News and Media, 29 Nov. 2017, https://www.independent.co.uk/news/world/americas/donald-trump-britain-first-video-twitter-posts-tweets-is-it-real-fake-jayda-fransen-true-us-president-a8082541.html.

213. Lenz , Ryan, and Booth Gunter. "100 Days in Trump's America." *Southern Poverty Law Center*, 27 Apr. 2017, https://www.splcenter.org/20170427/100-days-trumps-america.

214. Howard, Adam. "Trump Retweets Apparent Neo-Nazi for the Second Time This Year." *MSNBC*, NBCUniversal News Group, 11 Feb. 2016, https://www.msnbc.com/msnbc/trump-retweets-apparent-neo-nazi-the-second-time-year-msna793391.

215. Carless, Will. "They Spewed Hate. Then They Punctuated It with the President's Name." *The World* , 20 Apr. 2018, https://theworld.org/stories/2018-04-20/they-spewed-hate-then-they-punctuated-it-president-s-name.

216. Lee, Michelle Ye Hee. "Jeff Sessions's Comments on Race: For The Record." *The Washington Post*, WP Company, 2 Dec. 2016, https://www.washingtonpost.com/news/fact-checker/wp/2016/12/02/jeff-sessionss-comments-on-race-for-the-record/?utm_term=.16988fecbacf.

217. Harkinson, Josh. "Trump Selects a White Nationalist Leader as a Delegate in California." *Mother Jones*, 10 May 2016, https://www.motherjones.com/politics/2016/05/donald-trump-white-nationalist-afp-delegate-california/.

218. Cohler-Esses, Larry. "Exclusive: Sebastian Gorka's Ties to Nazi-Allied Group Stretch Back Decades." *The Forward*, 24 Apr. 2017, https://forward.com/news/369683/exclusive-sebastian-gorkas-ties-to-nazi-allied-group-stretch-back-decades/.

219. Detrow, Scott. "KKK Paper Endorses Trump; Campaign Calls Outlet 'Repulsive.'" *NPR*, 2 Nov. 2016, https://www.npr.org/2016/11/02/500352353/kkk-paper-endorses-trump-campaign-calls-outlet-repulsive.

220. Erickson, Amanda. "Adolf Hitler Also Published a List of Crimes Committed by Groups He Didn't Like." *The Washington Post*, WP Company, 2 Mar. 2017, https://www.washingtonpost.com/news/worldviews/wp/2017/03/02/adolf-hitler-also-published-a-list-of-crimes-committed-by-groups-he-didnt-like/.

221. McElwee, Sean, and Jason McDaniel. "Fear of Diversity Made People More Likely to Vote Trump." *The Nation*, 14 Mar. 2017, https://www.thenation.com/article/archive/fear-of-diversity-made-people-more-likely-to-vote-trump/.

222. Blumenthal, Paul, and JM Rieger. "This Stunningly Racist French Novel Is How Steve Bannon Explains the World." *HuffPost*, 4 Mar. 2017, https://www.huffpost.com/entry/

steve-bannon-camp-of-the-saints-immigration_n_58b75206e4b0284854b3dc03.

223. Krieg, Gregory. "A 28-Year-Old Democratic Socialist Just Ousted a Powerful, 10-Term Congressman in New York." *CNN*, CNN Politics, 27 June 2018, https://www.cnn.com/2018/06/26/politics/alexandria-ocasio-cortez-joe-crowley-new-york-14-primary/index.html.

224. Watkins, Eli. "First Muslim Women in Congress: Rashida Tlaib and Ilhan Omar." *CNN*, CNN Politics, 7 Nov. 2018, https://www.cnn.com/2018/11/06/politics/first-muslim-women-congress/index.html.

225. Resnick, Gideon. "There Will Now Likely Be Two Democratic Socialists of America Members in Congress." *The Daily Beast*, The Daily Beast Company, 9 Aug. 2018, https://www.thedailybeast.com/rashida-tlaib-alexandria-ocasio-cortez-dsa-democratic-socialists-of-america.

226. Ungar-Sargon, Batya. "Opinion: These Women of Color Are Poised to Make History in Congress. but What Does It Mean for Israel?" *The Forward*, 15 Aug. 2018, https://forward.com/opinion/408320/these-women-of-color-are-poised-to-make-history-in-congress-but-what-does/.

227. Nevel, Donna. "There Is No Such Thing as 'Progressive except Palestine'." *Mondoweiss*, 10 Jan. 2017, https://mondoweiss.net/2017/01/progressive-except-palestine/.

228. Elia, Nada. "Beto O'Rourke Is Anti-Trump and pro-Israel - Should Progressives Support Him?" *Mondoweiss*, 24 Sept. 2018, https://mondoweiss.net/2018/09/orourke-progressives-support/.

229. Stanley, Marc R. "It's Not Kosher to Say Beto O'Rourke Doesn't Support Israel." *The Jerusalem Post*, 20 Sept. 2018, https://www.jpost.com/Opinion/Its-not-kosher-to-say-Beto-ORourke-doesnt-support-Israel-567542.

230. Fernández, Belén. "Dead People Can't Take Selfies." *Jacobin*, 11 July 2014, https://www.jacobinmag.com/2014/07/dead-people-cant-take-selfies.

231. Shalom, Stephen R. "Aiding and Abetting Apartheid." *Jacobin*, 19 Sept. 2016, https://www.jacobinmag.com/2016/09/obama-israel-military-aid-netanyahu.

232. Shehada, Muhammad, and Jamie Stern-Weiner. "Debunking Four Myths Surrounding the Palestinian Protests." *VICE*, 28 June 2018, https://www.vice.com/en/article/7xm75d/debunking-four-myths-surrounding-the-palestinian-protests.

233. TOI staff. "58 Palestinians Said Killed, Including Terror Operatives, in Gaza Border Riots." *The Times of Israel*, 14 May 2018, https://www.timesofisrael.com/clashes-erupt-along-gaza-israel-border-ahead-of-us-embassy-inauguration/.

234. See note 232.

235. "Israel: 'Deliberate Attempts' by Military to Kill and Maim Gaza Protesters Continues." *Amnesty International UK*, 27 Apr. 2018, https://www.amnesty.org.uk/press-releases/israel-deliberate-attempts-military-kill-and-maim-gaza-protesters-continues.

236. Cunningham, Erin, and Hazem Balousha. "Scores of Palestinians Have Been Shot in Their Legs, and Some Face Amputation." *The Washington Post*, WP Company, 28 Apr. 2018, https://www.washingtonpost.com/news/world/wp/2018/04/28/feature/scores-of-palestinians-have-been-shot-in-their-legs-and-some-face-amputation/.

237. Finkelstein Jamie Stern-Weiner, Norman G., and Jamie Stern-Weiner. "Israel Has No Right of Self-Defense against Gaza." *Jacobin*, 27 July 2018, https://www.jacobinmag.com/2018/07/gaza-protests-israel-occupation-norman-finkelstein.

238. This was from a post on Norman Finkelstein's blog. The hyperlink no longer works and I was unable to find this post online while completing citations in February 2022.

239. Recommended introduction to this topic: Massad, Joseph. "Zionism, Anti-Semitism and Colonialism." *Al Jazeera*, 24 Dec. 2012, https://www.aljazeera.com/opinions/2012/12/24/zionism-anti-semitism-and-colonialism/.

240. Bennis, Phyllis. *Understanding the Palestinian-Israeli Conflict: A Primer*. Olive Branch Press, an Imprint of Interlink Publishing Group, Inc., 2019.

241. "UNRWA Releases Annual Report on Health of Palestine Refugees - Press Release - Question of Palestine." *United Nations*, 22 May 2018, https://www.un.org/unispal/document/unrwa-release-annual-report-on-health-of-palestine-refugees-unrwa-press-release/.

242. "FAQ on the Nakba: The Nakba and Palestinian Refugees Today." *Institute for Middle East Understanding (IMEU)*, 27 June 2012, https://imeu.org/article/faq-on-the-nakba-the-

nakba-and-palestinian-refugees-today.

243. Falk, Richard. "The inside Story on Our UN Report Calling Israel an Apartheid State." *The Nation*, 22 Mar. 2017, https://www.thenation.com/article/archive/the-inside-story-on-our-un-report-calling-israel-an-apartheid-state/.

244. Meehan, Maureen. "Israeli Textbooks and Children's Literature Promote Racism and Hatred toward Palestinians and Arabs." *Washington Report on Middle East Affairs (WRMEA)*, 17 May 2010, https://www.wrmea.org/1999-september/israeli-textbooks-and-childrens-literature-promote-racism-and-hatred-toward-palestinians-and-arabs.html.

245. "Empire Files: Israelis Speak Candidly to Abby Martin about Palestinians." *YouTube*, TeleSUR English, 1 Oct. 2017, https://youtu.be/1e_dbsVQrk4.

246. Abunimah, Ali. "Israeli Lawmaker's Call for Genocide of Palestinians Gets Thousands of Facebook Likes." *The Electronic Intifada*, 12 Feb. 2017, https://electronicintifada.net/blogs/ali-abunimah/israeli-lawmakers-call-genocide-palestinians-gets-thousands-facebook-likes.

247. "Palestinian Civil Society Call for BDS." *BDS Movement*, 9 July 2005, https://bdsmovement.net/call.

248. Abu-Manneh, Bashir. "The Occupation and BDS." *Jacobin*, 23 Apr. 2015, https://www.jacobinmag.com/2015/04/palestine-israel-bds-self-determination.

249. Abunimah, Ali. "'Tide Is Turning' as Natalie Portman Cancels Israel Appearance." *The Electronic Intifada*, 9 Apr. 2019, https://electronicintifada.net/blogs/ali-abunimah/tide-turning-natalie-portman-cancels-israel-appearance.

250. Barrows-Friedman, Nora. "Headliner Lana Del Rey Drops Out of Israel Music Festival." *The Electronic Intifada*, 9 Apr. 2018, https://electronicintifada.net/blogs/nora-barrows-friedman/headliner-lana-del-rey-drops-out-israel-music-festival.

251. Khalek, Rania. "Israel's Extermination of Whole Families in Gaza Reflects Genocidal Impulse." *The Electronic Intifada*, 12 Feb. 2017, https://electronicintifada.net/blogs/rania-khalek/israels-extermination-whole-families-gaza-reflects-genocidal-impulse.

252. Robinson, Jen [@suigenerisjen]. "Just Confirmed: #Assange Has Been Arrested Not Just for Breach of Bail Conditions but Also in Relation to a US Extradition Request. @Wikileaks @Khrafnsson." *Twitter*, 11 Apr. 2019, https://twitter.com/suigenerisjen/status/1116290879260639232.

253. Norton, Benjamin [@BenjaminNorton]. "Julian Assange's Lawyer: 'This Precedent Means That Any Journalist Can Be Extradited for Prosecution in the United States for Having Published Truthful Information about the United States'This Is an Attack on All of Us. If You're Silent, You're Complicit Pic.twitter.com/scv9SJoWsf." *Twitter*, 11 Apr. 2019, https://twitter.com/BenjaminNorton/status/1116374557936574464.

254. "Baghdad War Diary." *Wikileaks*, https://wikileaks.org/irq/.

255. McGreal, Chris. "Wikileaks Reveals Video Showing US Air Crew Shooting Down Iraqi Civilians." *The Guardian*, Guardian News and Media, 5 Apr. 2010, https://www.theguardian.com/world/2010/apr/05/wikileaks-us-army-iraq-attack.

256. Solomon, Norman. "The Military-Industrial-Media Complex." *FAIR*, 1 Aug. 2005, https://fair.org/extra/the-military-industrial-media-complex/.

257. "What's Wrong with the News?" *FAIR*, 8 Nov. 2019, https://fair.org/about-fair/whats-wrong-with-the-news/.

258. Shafer, Jack. "The Spies Who Came in to the TV Studio." *POLITICO Magazine*, 6 Feb. 2018, https://www.politico.com/magazine/story/2018/02/06/john-brennan-james-clapper-michael-hayden-former-cia-media-216943/.

259. Suellentrop, Chris. "The TV Generals." *Slate Magazine*, Slate, 26 Mar. 2003, https://slate.com/news-and-politics/2003/03/the-tv-generals.html.

260. "The Six Words That Got Marc Lamont Hill Fired from CNN." *Al Jazeera*, The Listening Post, 9 Dec. 2018, https://www.aljazeera.com/program/the-listening-post/2018/12/9/the-six-words-that-got-marc-lamont-hill-fired-from-cnn.

261. "Phil Donahue on His 2003 Firing from MSNBC, When Liberal Network Couldn't Tolerate Antiwar Voices." *YouTube*, Democracy Now!, 21 Mar. 2013, https://youtu.be/ozxzNjRqCiE.

262. Hayes, Chris [@chrislhayes]. "Hold on, Currently Writing a One Act Play Set in a Federal Prison with Assange and Avenatti as Cellmates." *Twitter*, 11 Apr. 2019, https://twitter.

com/chrislhayes/status/1116352724818382848.

263. Robinson, Nathan. "Many Democrats and Liberals Are Cheering Assange's Arrest. That's Foolish | Nathan Robinson." *The Guardian*, Guardian News and Media, 14 Apr. 2019, https://www.theguardian.com/commentisfree/2019/apr/14/democrats-liberals-assange.

264. Jones, Owen. "Why Are Liberals Now Cheerleading a Warmongering Trump?" *The Guardian*, Guardian News and Media, 9 Apr. 2017, https://www.theguardian.com/commentisfree/2017/apr/09/liberals-donald-trump-syria-missile-strikes.

265. MacLeod, Alan. "'Resistance' Media Side with Trump to Promote Coup in Venezuela." *FAIR*, 25 Jan. 2019, https://fair.org/home/resistance-media-side-with-trump-to-promote-coup-in-venezuela/.

266. Marcetic, Branko. "Before the Hurricane." *Jacobin*, 30 Aug. 2017, https://jacobinmag.com/2017/08/hurricane-harvey-cuba-disaster-plan.

267. "Cuba: The New Constitution Comes into Force Today." *TeleSUR English*, TeleSUR, 10 Apr. 2019, https://www.telesurenglish.net/news/Cuba-The-New-Constitution-Comes-Into-Force-Today-20190410-0008.html.

268. "Cuba Passes Electoral Law, Reinstates Role of Prime Minister." *TeleSUR English*, TeleSUR, 15 July 2019, https://www.telesurenglish.net/news/cuba-new-electoral-law-role-of-prime-minister-miguel-diaz-canel-20190715-0011.html.

269. Jacomino, Pavel. "Role of Foreign Investment Recognized in New Cuban Constitution." *Radio Havana Cuba*, 8 Jan. 2019, https://www.radiohc.cu/en/noticias/nacionales/180540-role-of-foreign-investment-recognized-in-new-cuban-constitution.

270. "What Do You Need to Know about Sunday's Cuban Referendum?" *TeleSUR English*, TeleSUR, 22 Feb. 2019, https://www.telesurenglish.net/news/What-Do-You-Need-to-Know-About-Sundays-Cuban-Referendum--20190222-0014.html.

271. Jacomino, Pavel. "Popular Consultation on Cuban Constitution Enters Final Week." *Radio Havana Cuba*, 12 Nov. 2018, https://www.radiohc.cu/en/noticias/nacionales/176339-popular-consultation-on-cuban-constitution-enters-final-week.

272. "86% Votes for New Constitution in Cuba." *TeleSUR English*, 25 Feb. 2019, https://www.telesurenglish.net/news/86-Votes-For-New-Constitution-in-Cuba--20190225-0014.html.

273. Shupak, Gregory. "US Media Erase Years of Chavismo's Gains." *FAIR*, 20 Feb. 2019, https://fair.org/home/us-media-erase-years-of-chavismos-gains/.

274. Grandin, Greg. "On the Legacy of Hugo Chávez." *The Nation*, 29 June 2015, https://www.thenation.com/article/archive/legacy-hugo-chavez/.

275. Embassy of Venezuela in the US. "Constitutional Reforms in Venezuela." *Venezuelanalysis.com*, 26 Oct. 2007, https://venezuelanalysis.com/analysis/2764.

276. Withers, Matt. "John Bolton and the Monroe Doctrine." *The Economist*, The Economist Newspaper, 11 May 2019, https://www.economist.com/leaders/2019/05/09/john-bolton-and-the-monroe-doctrine.

277. Levy, Arturo Lopez. "Why Trump's Cuba Policy Is so Wrong." *NACLA*, 20 May 2019, https://nacla.org/news/2019/05/27/why-trump%E2%80%99s-cuba-policy-so-wrong.

278. Landau, Saul. "Cuba: A Half-Century of Distorted News and Counting . . ." *NACLA*, 16 May 2008, https://nacla.org/news/cuba-half-century-distorted-news-and-counting.

279. Norton, Ben. "US Coup in Venezuela Motivated by Oil and Corporate Interests - Militarist John Bolton Spills the Beans." *The Grayzone*, 29 Jan. 2019, https://thegrayzone.com/2019/01/29/us-coup-venezuela-oil-corporate-john-bolton/.

280. Curcio, Pascualina. "Venezuela: Is President Maduro 'Illegitimate'? 10 Facts to Counter the Lies." *Green Left*, 25 Jan. 2019, https://www.greenleft.org.au/content/venezuela-president-maduro-illegitimate-10-facts-counter-lies.

281. Cohen, Dan, and Max Blumenthal. "The Making of Juan Guaidó: How the US Regime Change Laboratory Created Venezuela's Coup Leader." *The Grayzone*, 29 Jan. 2019, https://thegrayzone.com/2019/01/29/the-making-of-juan-guaido-how-the-us-regime-change-laboratory-created-venezuelas-coup-leader/.

282. Norton, Ben. "'It's Our Backyard!': Bill Maher Cheers US-Led Coup in Venezuela in Unhinged Colonial Tirade." *The Grayzone*, 26 Jan. 2019, https://thegrayzone.com/2019/01/26/bill-maher-us-coup-venezuela-neocolonial-backyard/.

283. Forero, Juan. "Documents Show C.I.A. Knew of a Coup Plot in Venezuela." *The*

New York Times, 3 Dec. 2004, https://www.nytimes.com/2004/12/03/washington/world/documents-show-cia-knew-of-a-coup-plot-in-venezuela.html.

284. Weisbrot, Mark, and Jeffery Sachs. "Economic Sanctions as Collective Punishment: The Case of Venezuela." *Center for Economic Policy Research*, Apr. 2019, https://cepr.net/images/stories/reports/venezuela-sanctions-2019-04.pdf.

285. The Foreign Ministry of the Bolivarian Republic of Venezuela. "Venezuela: Cuban Revolution 'Will Continue to Light the Way during This Challenging and Complex 21st Century.'" *Venezuelanalysis.com*, 2 Jan. 2019, https://venezuelanalysis.com/news/14199.

286. "Venezuela Welcomes 2,500 Cuban Doctors Leaving Brazil." *Venezuelanalysis.com*, TeleSUR English, 14 Jan. 2019, https://venezuelanalysis.com/news/14217.

287. "Worldwide Solidarity Rallies Held in Support of Venezuela." *Venezuelanalysis.com*, TeleSUR English, 12 Aug. 2019, https://venezuelanalysis.com/news/14623.

288. Striffler, Steve. "Opinion: Venezuela, US Solidarity, and the Future of Socialism." *Common Dreams*, 26 Mar. 2019, https://www.commondreams.org/views/2019/03/26/venezuela-us-solidarity-and-future-socialism.

289. Block, Diana. "The Venceremos Brigade at 50." *MR Online*, Monthly Review, 14 Sept. 2019, https://mronline.org/2019/09/24/the-venceremos-brigade-at-50/.

290. "DC Cops Arrest Journalist After Venezuela Reporting." *YouTube*, The Jimmy Dore Show, 2 Nov. 2019, https://youtu.be/q2WHqnxjfx4.

291. "Journalist Max Blumenthal Arrested on False Charge in DC." *YouTube*, The Grayzone, 3 Nov. 2019.

292. Norton, Ben. "'This Charge Is 100% False': Grayzone Editor Max Blumenthal Arrested Months after Reporting on Venezuelan Opposition Violence." *The Grayzone*, 28 Oct. 2019, https://thegrayzone.com/2019/10/28/this-charge-is-one-hundred-percent-false-grayzone-editor-max-blumenthal-arrested-months-after-reporting-on-venezuelan-opposition-violence/.

293. Emersberger, Joe. "Max Blumenthal's Arrest Exposes the Limits of Press Freedom." *Truthdig*, 31 Oct. 2019, https://www.truthdig.com/articles/max-blumenthals-arrest-exposes-the-limits-of-press-freedom/.

294. Gosztola, Kevin. "Journalist Max Blumenthal Arrested and Charged in Political Prosecution." *Shadowproof*, 28 Oct. 2019, https://shadowproof.com/2019/10/28/journalist-max-blumenthal-arrested-charged-venezuela-embassy-reporting/.

295. See note 292.

296. Muhawesh, Mnar. "Mintpress, Grayzone Journalists Endure Us Govt Blackout and Siege at Venezuelan Embassy in DC." *The Grayzone*, 9 May 2019, https://thegrayzone.com/2019/05/09/mintpress-grayzone-journalists-us-blackout-siege-venezuelan-embassy-dc/.

297. Sprague, Jeb, and Alexander Rubinstein. "Who's behind the pro-Guaidó Crowd Besieging the Venezuelan Embassy?" *MintPress News*, 17 May 2019, https://www.mintpressnews.com/whos-behind-the-pro-guaido-crowd-besieging-venezuelan-embassy-in-dc/258533/.

298. "NLG IC Statement on the Arrest of Max Blumenthal, the Attack on Venezuela and the Repression of Dissent." *National Lawyers Guild International Committee*, 28 Oct. 2019, https://nlginternational.org/2019/10/nlg-ic-statement-on-the-arrest-of-max-blumenthal-the-attack-on-venezuela-and-the-repression-of-dissent/.

299. See note 293.

300. Gottesdiener, Laura. "10 Brilliant Quotes by Noam Chomsky on How Media Really Operates in America." *Alternet*, 6 Dec. 2012, https://www.alternet.org/2012/12/10-brilliant-quotes-noam-chomsky-how-media-really-operates-america/.

301. "CIA Agents Turned MSM Pundits." *Facebook Watch*, Soapbox, 3 Oct. 2019, https://www.facebook.com/watch/?v=2377599642479115.

302. Johnson, Adam. "Your Complete Guide to the N.Y. Times' Support of U.s.-Backed Coups in Latin America." *Truthdig*, 29 Jan. 2019, https://www.truthdig.com/articles/your-complete-guide-to-the-n-y-times-support-of-u-s-backed-coups-in-latin-america/.

303. Nichols, John. "The House Impeaches Trump." *The Nation*, 19 Dec. 2019, https://www.thenation.com/article/archive/impeachment-vote-third-president/.

304. Blumenthal, Max. "The US Is Arming and Assisting Neo-Nazis in Ukraine, While Congress Debates Prohibition." *The Grayzone*, 7 Apr. 2018, https://thegrayzone.

com/2018/04/07/the-us-is-arming-and-assisting-neo-nazis-in-ukraine-while-congress-debates-prohibition/.

305. Cortright, David. "A Hard Look at Iraq Sanctions." *The Nation*, 14 Jan. 2020, https://www.thenation.com/article/archive/hard-look-iraq-sanctions/.

306. Robinson, Nathan J. "Bill Clinton's Act of Terrorism." *Jacobin*, 12 Oct. 2016, https://www.jacobinmag.com/2016/10/bill-clinton-al-shifa-sudan-bombing-khartoum/.

307. Robers, Dan. "Wall Street Deregulation Pushed by Clinton Advisers, Documents Reveal." *The Guardian*, Guardian News and Media, 19 Apr. 2014, https://www.theguardian.com/world/2014/apr/19/wall-street-deregulation-clinton-advisers-obama.

308. Gilens, Martin, and Benjamin I. Page. 2014, *Testing Theories of American Politics: Elites, Interest Groups, and Average Citizens*, https://www.cambridge.org/core/services/aop-cambridge-core/content/view/62327F513959D0A304D4893B382B992B/S1537592714001595a.pdf/testing_theories_of_american_politics_elites_interest_groups_and_average_citizens.pdf. Accessed 7 Jan. 2022.

309. Monbiot, George. "Neoliberalism: The Deep Story That Lies beneath Donald Trump's Triumph." *The Guardian*, Guardian News and Media, 14 Nov. 2016, https://www.theguardian.com/commentisfree/2016/nov/14/neoliberalsim-donald-trump-george-monbiot.

310. Reich, Robert. "Almost 80% of US Workers Live from Paycheck to Paycheck. Here's Why." *The Guardian*, Guardian News and Media, 29 July 2018, https://www.theguardian.com/commentisfree/2018/jul/29/us-economy-workers-paycheck-robert-reich.

311. Bruenig, Matt. "The Real Costs of the U.S. Health-Care Mess." *The Atlantic*, Atlantic Media Company, 9 Aug. 2019, https://www.theatlantic.com/ideas/archive/2019/08/best-democratic-health-plan/595657/.

312. Himmelstein, David U., and Steffie Woolhandler. "Medical Bankruptcy Is Real, Even If the Washington Post Refuses to Believe It." *Bernie Sanders Official Website*, https://berniesanders.com/medical-bankruptcy/.

313. "Federal Reserve Board Issues Report on the Economic Well-Being of U.S. Households." *Board of Governors of the Federal Reserve System*, 19 May 2017, https://www.federalreserve.gov/newsevents/pressreleases/other20170519a.htm.

314. Sanders, Bernie. "Bernie Sanders: America Is Drowning in Student Debt. Here's My Plan to End It." *Fortune*, 9 July 2019, https://fortune.com/2019/07/09/bernie-sanders-cancel-student-debt/.

315. This figure has been updated since the piece was written.

316. "Student Loan Snapshot - Consumer Financial Protection Bureau." *Consumer Financial Protection Bureau*, Jan. 2017, https://files.consumerfinance.gov/f/documents/201701_cfpb_OA-Student-Loan-Snapshot.pdf.

317. O'Donovan, Caroline. "People Are Using Ubers as Ambulances - and Drivers Hate It." *BuzzFeed News*, 26 Feb. 2018, https://www.buzzfeednews.com/article/carolineodonovan/taking-uber-lyft-emergency-room-legal-liabilities.

318. Gagliardo-Silver, Victoria. "Americans Driving to Canada for Cheaper Insulin as Prices Skyrocket." *The Independent*, Independent Digital News and Media, 11 May 2019, https://www.independent.co.uk/news/world/americas/us-insulin-prices-rise-canada-border-cost-a8909921.html.

319. "Why America's Drinking Water Crisis Goes beyond Flint." *BBC News*, BBC, 28 Nov. 2017, https://www.bbc.com/news/av/world-us-canada-42141519.

320. Kochhar, Rakesh, and Anthony Cilluffo. "How U.S. Wealth Inequality Has Changed since Great Recession." *Pew Research Center*, 1 Nov. 2017, https://www.pewresearch.org/fact-tank/2017/11/01/how-wealth-inequality-has-changed-in-the-u-s-since-the-great-recession-by-race-ethnicity-and-income/.

321. Benns, Whitney. "American Slavery, Reinvented." *The Atlantic*, Atlantic Media Company, 21 Sept. 2015, https://www.theatlantic.com/business/archive/2015/09/prison-labor-in-america/406177/.

322. DeSilver, Drew. "For Most Americans, Real Wages Have Barely Budged for Decades." *Pew Research Center*, 7 Aug. 2018, https://www.pewresearch.org/fact-tank/2018/08/07/for-most-us-workers-real-wages-have-barely-budged-for-decades/.

323. "The Productivity–Pay Gap." *Economic Policy Institute*, Aug. 2021, https://www.epi.org/productivity-pay-gap/.

324. Sanders, Katie. "Bernie Sanders Says 99 Percent of 'New' Income Is Going to Top 1 Percent." *PolitiFact*, 19 Apr. 2015, https://www.politifact.com/factchecks/2015/apr/19/bernie-s/bernie-sanders-says-99-percent-new-income-going-to/.

325. Puzzanghera, Jim. "A Decade after the Financial Crisis, Many Americans Are Still Struggling to Recover." *The Seattle Times*, The Seattle Times Company, 10 Sept. 2018, https://www.seattletimes.com/nation-world/a-decade-after-the-financial-crisis-many-americans-are-still-struggling-to-recover/.

326. Cohn, Jonathan. "Centrist Pundits Assume Voters Agree with Them. Polling Tells a Different Story." *In These Times*, 15 Nov. 2019, https://inthesetimes.com/article/centrism-progressive-democrats-green-new-deal-medicare-for-all-pelosi-chait.

327. Mair, Liz. "Do Voters Vote on Policy (Elizabeth Warren) or Personality (Joe Biden)?" *Washington Examiner*, 26 Aug. 2019, https://www.washingtonexaminer.com/tag/joe-biden?source=%2Fopinion%2Fdo-voters-vote-on-policy-elizabeth-warren-or-personality-joe-biden.

328. Source for the first three bullet points: "Very Clear & Simple Reasons To Vote Bernie Over Warren." *YouTube*, Secular Talk, 23 Sept. 2019, https://www.youtube.com/watch?v=ZZbJQx5fpcw.

329. Krieger, Sonja. "Elizabeth Warren Votes for Massive Increase of War Budget." *Left Voice*, 2 Oct. 2017, https://www.leftvoice.org/Elizabeth-Warren-Votes-for-Massive-Increase-of-War-Budget/.

330. "My First Term Plan for Reducing Health Care Costs in America." *Elizabethwarren.com*, https://elizabethwarren.com/plans/m4a-transition.

331. Smith, Allan. "Sanders Draws Line between Himself and Warren: A 'Capitalist to Her Bones'." *NBCNews.com*, NBCUniversal News Group, 13 Oct. 2019, https://www.nbcnews.com/politics/2020-election/sanders-draws-line-between-himself-warren-capitalist-her-bones-n1065526.

332. Edwards, Haley Sweetland. "Elizabeth Warren Thinks the U.S. Is Ready for Her 2020 Ideas." *Time*, 9 May 2019, https://time.com/longform/elizabeth-warren-2020/.

333. Golshan, Tara. "Bernie Sanders's Real Base Is Diverse - and Very Young." *Vox*, 7 Mar. 2019, https://www.vox.com/2019/3/7/18216899/bernie-sanders-bro-base-polling-2020-president.

334. "Campaign Update from Iowa." *YouTube*, Bernie Sanders, 30 Dec. 2019, https://youtu.be/5KZ3MKraNKYs.

335. Marcetic, Branko. "The Bernie Sanders Origin Story, Part 1." *Jacobin*, 11 Dec. 2019, https://jacobinmag.com/2019/12/bernie-sanders-vermont-mayor-history-elections.

336. "The Green New Deal." *Bernie Sanders Official Website*, https://berniesanders.com/issues/green-new-deal/.

337. Revesz, Rachael. "Survey finds Hillary Clinton has 'more than 99% chance' of winning election over Donald Trump

338. Day, Meagan, and Matt Karp. "Bernie Is the Candidate Who Can Beat Trump. Here's Why." *Jacobin*, 20 Dec. 2019, https://www.jacobinmag.com/2019/12/bernie-sanders-vs-donald-trump.

339. Nagle, Rebecca. "Elizabeth Warren Has Spent Her Adult Life Repeating a Lie. I Want Her to Tell the Truth." *HuffPost*, 23 Aug. 2019, https://www.huffpost.com/entry/elizabeth-warren-cherokee-apology_n_5d5ed7e6e4b0dfcbd48a1b01.

340. Fenwick, Cody. "Elizabeth Warren Admits She Used to Be a Republican - Here's Why She Abandoned the Party." *Salon*, 23 Apr. 2019, https://www.salon.com/2019/04/23/elizabeth-warren-admits-she-used-to-be-a-republican-heres-why-she-abandoned-the-party_partner/.

341. Grim, Ryan. "The Critical Moment of Pete Buttigieg's Political Career." *The Intercept*, 20 Sept. 2019, https://theintercept.com/2019/09/20/pete-buttigieg-south-bend-police/.

342. Grim, Ryan. "The Problem with Pete Buttigieg's 'Douglass Plan' for Black America." *The Intercept*, 15 Nov. 2019, https://theintercept.com/2019/11/15/pete-buttigieg-campaign-black-voters/.

343. Ward, Alex. "Senate Passes Resolution to End US Role in Yemen War." *Vox*, 13 Mar. 2019, https://www.vox.com/2019/3/13/18263894/yemen-war-senate-sanders-murphy-lee.

344. Camp, Lee. "Trump's Military Drops a Bomb Every 12 Minutes, and No One Is

Talking about It." *Truthdig*, 9 June 2018, https://www.truthdig.com/articles/trumps-military-drops-a-bomb-every-12-minutes-and-no-one-is-talking-about-it/.

345. "A New Year and a New Trump Foreign Policy Blunder in Iraq." *CODEPINK*, https://www.codepink.org/a_new_year_and_a_new_trump_foreign_policy_blunder_in_iraq.

346. Sanders, Bernie. "How to Fight Antisemitism." *Jewish Currents*, 11 Nov. 2019, https://jewishcurrents.org/how-to-fight-antisemitism/.

347. Holmes, Jack. "An Expert on Concentration Camps Says That's Exactly What the U.S. Is Running at the Border." *Esquire*, 13 June 2019, https://www.esquire.com/news-politics/a27813648/concentration-camps-southern-border-migrant-detention-facilities-trump/.

348. See note 346.

349. Krieg, Gregory. "Sanders Stands by Castro Comments, Knocks Democratic Critics." *CNN*, Cable News Network, 24 Feb. 2020, https://www.cnn.com/politics/live-news/2020-democratic-town-hall-south-carolina-monday/h_6b2b32bce628fa70c47d1b57b9cb282c.

350. "Bernie Sanders Stands by His Qualified Praise of Fidel Castro's Regime in Cuba: "(Castro) Went out and They Helped People Learn to Read and Write. You Know What, I Think Teaching People to Read and Write Is a Good Thing' Https://T.co/Weidzkkvfb #Cnntownhall Pic.twitter.com/Yjlludapde." *Twitter*, CNN, 24 Feb. 2020, https://twitter.com/CNN/status/1232157903756369921?s=20&t=0kDKiCUWQ-xJzdIfxhCR-Q.

351. Mark, Monica. "Cuba Leads Fight against Ebola in Africa as West Frets about Border Security." *The Guardian*, Guardian News and Media, 11 Oct. 2014, https://www.theguardian.com/world/2014/oct/12/cuba-leads-fights-against-ebola-africa.

352. Kaczynski, Andrew. "7 Nelson Mandela Quotes You Probably Won't See in the U.S. Media." *BuzzFeed News*, 6 Dec. 2013, https://www.buzzfeednews.com/article/andrewkaczynski/7-nelson-mandela-quotes-you-probably-wont-see-in-the-us-medi.

353. LeBrun, Aren R [@proustmalone]. "Watch: In 1991, after Being Freed from Prison, Nelson Mandela Met with Fidel Castro to Thank Him for His Aid in the Fight against Apartheid.Mandela Called the Cuban Revolution 'a Source of Inspiration for All Freedom Loving People.' Why Does @Petebuttigieg Hate Nelson Mandela? Pic.twitter.com/l7zchkxxva." *Twitter*, 25 Feb. 2020, https://twitter.com/proustmalone/status/1232323475303518209?s=20&t=atEYIZJad1CEkNxn2-FelA.

354. Grillo, Ioan. "Cuba Has Had a Lung Cancer Vaccine for Years." *The World*, https://theworld.org/stories/cuba-has-had-lung-cancer-vaccine-years. Accessed 20 Feb. 2022.

355. Worland, Justin. "Mother to Child HIV Transmission: Cuba Eliminates HIV in Newborns." *Time*, 1 July 2015, https://time.com/3943045/cuba-hiv-mother-daughter/.

356. "Cuba Starts Giving out Free Preventive HIV Pill." *OnCubaNews English*, 5 Apr. 2019, https://oncubanews.com/en/cuba/cuba-starts-giving-out-free-preventive-hiv-pill/.

357. "Cuba Has 9 Doctors per 1000 Citizens, Highest in Its History." *TeleSUR English*, TeleSUR, 23 July 2019, https://www.telesurenglish.net/news/cuba-cuban-doctors-highest-number-in-history-20190723-0009.html.

358. "Health Situation in the Americas: Basic Indicators 2012." *Pan American Health Organization*, World Health Organization, 2012, http://ais.paho.org/chi/brochures/2012/BI_2012_ENG.pdf.

359. Marcetic, Branko. "Before the Hurricane." *Jacobin*, 30 Aug. 2017, https://jacobinmag.com/2017/08/hurricane-harvey-cuba-disaster-plan.

360. Thorbecke, Catherine. "US Death Toll From Hurricane Matthew Climbs to 44." *ABC News*, ABC News Network, 14 Oct. 2016, https://abcnews.go.com/US/us-death-toll-hurricane-matthew-climbs-42/story?id=42807375.

361. See note 359.

362. Grim, Ryan. "Bernie Sanders Ends Presidential Run." *The Intercept*, 8 Apr. 2020, https://theintercept.com/2020/04/08/bernie-sanders-drops-out/.

363. This hyperlink no longer worked when I was in the process of completing citations. The previous URL was: https://www.sanders.senate.gov/legislative-landmarks

364. Matthew John. "25 Reasons Joe Biden Isn't Necessarily 'Better than Trump.'" *Medium*, Fourth Wave, 8 Mar. 2020, https://thisamericanleft.medium.com/25-reasons-joe-biden-shouldnt-be-president-6036a87feb6d.

365. Palma, Bethania. "Did Biden Say He Didn't Want His Kids Growing up in a 'Racial Jungle'?" *Snopes.com*, 10 Mar. 2020, https://www.snopes.com/fact-check/biden-racial-jungle-

quote/.

366. Gomez, Henry J., and Darren Sands. "Joe Biden Once Spoke at Strom Thurmond's Memorial Service. How Do People Feel about That Now?" *BuzzFeed News*, 17 Feb. 2019, https://www.buzzfeednews.com/article/henrygomez/joe-biden-strom-thurmond-eulogy.

367. Matthew John. "Is #MeToo Finally Catching up with Joe Biden?" *Medium*, Dialogue & Discourse, 25 Mar. 2020, https://medium.com/discourse/is-metoo-finally-catching-up-with-joe-biden-1354b640870.

368. Bruenig, Matt, and Ryan Cooper. "How Obama Destroyed Black Wealth." *Jacobin*, 7 Dec. 2017, https://jacobinmag.com/2017/12/obama-foreclosure-crisis-wealth-inequality.

369. Marshall, Serena. "Obama Has Deported More People Than Any Other President." *ABC News*, ABC News Network, 29 Aug. 2016, https://abcnews.go.com/Politics/obamas-deportation-policy-numbers/story?id=41715661.

370. Palma, Bethania. "Did Obama Admin Build Cages That House Immigrant Children at U.s.-Mexico Border?" *Snopes*, 2 July 2019, https://www.snopes.com/fact-check/obama-build-cages-immigrants/.

371. "Intercepted Podcast: The Espionage Axe - Donald Trump and the War against a Free Press." *The Intercept*, 15 May 2019, https://theintercept.com/2019/05/15/the-espionage-axe-donald-trump-and-the-war-against-a-free-press/.

372. Purkiss, Jessica, and Jack Serle. "Obama's Covert Drone War in Numbers: Ten Times More Strikes than Bush." *The Bureau of Investigative Journalism*, 17 Jan. 2017, https://www.thebureauinvestigates.com/stories/2017-01-17/obamas-covert-drone-war-in-numbers-ten-times-more-strikes-than-bush.

373. Scahill, Jeremy. "Leaked Military Documents Expose the Inner Workings of Obama's Drone Wars." *The Intercept*, 15 Oct. 2015, https://theintercept.com/drone-papers/the-assassination-complex/.

374. "Is It Legal for the U.S. to Kill a 16-Year-Old U.S. Citizen with a Drone?" *Amnesty International USA*, 20 July 2012, https://www.amnestyusa.org/is-it-legal-for-the-u-s-to-kill-a-16-year-old-u-s-citizen-with-a-drone/.

375. See note 373.

376. Johnston, Jake. "How Pentagon Officials May Have Encouraged a 2009 Coup in Honduras." *The Intercept*, 29 Aug. 2017, https://theintercept.com/2017/08/29/honduras-coup-us-defense-departmetnt-center-hemispheric-defense-studies-chds/.

377. Cohen, Stephen F. "America's Collusion with Neo-Nazis." *The Nation*, 2 May 2018, https://www.thenation.com/article/archive/americas-collusion-with-neo-nazis/.

378. Emmons, Alex. "Obama Opens NSA's Vast Trove of Warrantless Data to Entire Intelligence Community, Just in Time for Trump." *The Intercept*, 13 Jan. 2017, https://theintercept.com/2017/01/13/obama-opens-nsas-vast-trove-of-warrantless-data-to-entire-intelligence-community-just-in-time-for-trump/.

379. Magane, Azmia. "Obama's Drone Warfare Is Something We Need to Talk About." *Teen Vogue*, 2 June 2017, https://www.teenvogue.com/story/obamas-drone-warfare-is-something-we-need-to-talk-about.

380. Shupak, Greg. "The Disaster in Libya." *Jacobin*, 9 Feb. 2015, https://www.jacobinmag.com/2015/02/libya-intervention-nato-imperialism/.

381. Norton, Ben. "Media Erase NATO Role in Bringing Slave Markets to Libya." *FAIR*, 28 Nov. 2017, https://fair.org/home/media-nato-regime-change-war-libya-slave-markets/.

382. Webb, Whitney. "Sex Slavery, Isis & Illegal Arms Trade: Libya Plunged into Failed State after US Invasion." *MintPress News*, 4 May 2017, https://www.mintpressnews.com/sex-slavery-isis-illegal-arms-trade-libya-plunged-failed-state-us-invasion/227478/.

383. Jacobson, Louis. "Politifact - Obama Says Heritage Foundation Is Source of Health Exchange Idea." *PolitiFact*, 1 Apr. 2010, https://www.politifact.com/factchecks/2010/apr/01/barack-obama/obama-says-heritage-foundation-source-health-excha/.

384. Jacobins Editors. "Assessing Obama." *Jacobin*, 20 Jan. 2017, https://www.jacobinmag.com/2017/01/barack-obama-presidency-trump-inauguration/.

385. Diavolo, Lucy. "Michelle Obama Defending George W. Bush Is a Lesson in Class Solidarity." *Teen Vogue*, 11 Dec. 2019, https://www.teenvogue.com/story/michelle-obama-defending-george-w-bush-lesson-class-solidarity.

386. Grahame-Smith, Seth [@sethgs]. "'Never Biden' = a Vote for Trump 'I'm Voting

Green Party' = a Vote for Trump' Write in Bernie' = a Vote for Trump' Meh I'll Stay Home' = a Vote for Trump If You're a Trump Voter, Own It. but Don't Dress It up as a Protest." *Twitter*, 8 Apr. 2020, https://twitter.com/sethgs/status/1247962546658660352?s=20&t=XGDeStWWjiWYPIljkiSoA.

387. Hasan, Mehdi [@mehdirhasan]. "Just a Warning: I Have No Tolerance for People Telling Me That They're OK with a 2nd Trump Term or That 'They're All the Same'. Some of Us, Especially Those of Us Who Are Muslims and Immigrants, Don't Have Your Privilege. so Unfollow Me, or Prepare to Be Slammed and/or Blocked." *Twitter*, 9 Apr. 2020, https://twitter.com/mehdirhasan/status/1248322611563704321?s=20&t=wfoCZ1NXIlhRV4g5D8ETog.

388. Saeed, Sana [@SanaSaeed]. "The People I See Espousing a Non-Voting Perspective Are Mainly Brown, Black, Immigrant Low-Income Voters; Many Are People without Healthcare, in Student Debt. It's Not Always a Privilege to Exercise the Choice to Not Vote: Often It's Rooted in Manufactured Disenfranchisement." *Twitter*, 9 Apr. 2020, https://twitter.com/SanaSaeed/status/1248352770752741377?s=20&t=RVmifR_Wa_mCQ21LG81OaQ.

389. Greenwald, Glenn. "Nonvoters Are Not Privileged." *The Intercept*, 9 Apr. 2020, https://theintercept.com/2020/04/09/nonvoters-are-not-privileged-they-are-largely-lower-income-non-white-and-dissatisfied-with-the-two-parties/.

390. Milano, Alyssa [@Alyssa_Milano]. "He Wants to Forgive Student Debt.he Wants to Expand Medicare, More Generous Subsidies and Medicaid Funding along with a Public Option to Achieve Universal Health Care.$2 Trillion in New Spending on Early Education, Post-Secondary Education, and Housing.#Whyimvotingforjoe." *Twitter*, 11 Apr. 2020, https://twitter.com/Alyssa_Milano/status/1248811034254565376?s=20&t=LLzslBDl4MIU0XXRtMyuag.

391. Chait, Jonathan. "Joe Biden's Platform Is More Progressive than You Think." *Intelligencer*, 12 Mar. 2020, https://nymag.com/intelligencer/2020/03/joe-biden-platform-progressive-health-care-climate-taxes.html.

392. Murphy, Tim. "House of Cards." *Mother Jones*, 11 Nov. 2019, https://www.motherjones.com/politics/2019/11/biden-bankruptcy-president/.

393. Teachout, Zephyr. "'Middle Class' Joe Biden Has a Corruption Problem – It Makes Him a Weak Candidate." *The Guardian*, Guardian News and Media, 20 Jan. 2020, https://www.theguardian.com/commentisfree/2020/jan/20/joe-biden-corruption-donald-trump.

394. Higginbotham, Tim. "Joe Lie-Den." *Jacobin*, 6 Sept. 2019, https://jacobinmag.com/2019/09/joe-biden-lies-gaffes-climate-townhall-democratic-race-2020.

395. Savage, Luke. "Joe Biden Keeps Lying - but You Won't Hear It from Liberal Media." *Jacobin*, 30 Mar. 2020, https://www.jacobinmag.com/2020/03/joe-biden-mainstream-media-lies-trust-reporting.

396. King, Shaun. "2 Truths and 31 Lies Joe Biden Has Told about His Work in the Civil Rights Movement." *Shaun King's Substack*, 29 Jan. 2020, https://shaunking.substack.com/p/2-truths-and-31-lies-joe-biden-has?utm_source=url.

397. Satija, Neena. "Echoes of Biden's 1987 Plagiarism Scandal Continue to Reverberate." *The Washington Post*, WP Company, 5 June 2019, https://www.washingtonpost.com/investigations/echoes-of-bidens-1987-plagiarism-scandal-continue-to-reverberate/2019/06/05/dbaf3716-7292-11e9-9eb4-0828f5389013_story.html.

398. "The Struggle Continues." *YouTube*, Bernie Sanders, 9 Apr. 2020, https://youtu.be/Oi4pCuUVSWQ.

399. "To Millennials Who Think They Have It Tough: 'Give Me a Break,' Biden Says." *Los Angeles Times*, 11 Jan. 2018, https://www.latimes.com/95641832-132.html.

400. Halper, Katie. "Joe Biden's Campaign Claimed It Was Safe to Vote during the Pandemic. It Absolutely Wasn't." *Jacobin*, 31 Mar. 2020, https://jacobinmag.com/2020/03/joe-biden-bernie-sanders-coronavirus-primary-voting.

401. Gertz, Bill. "Coronavirus Link to China Biowarfare Program Possible, Analyst Says." *The Washington Times*, 26 Jan. 2020, https://www.washingtontimes.com/news/2020/jan/26/coronavirus-link-to-china-biowarfare-program-possi/.

402. Rogin, Josh. "Opinion | State Department Cables Warned of Safety Issues at Wuhan Lab Studying Bat Coronaviruses." *The Washington Post*, WP Company, 20 Apr. 2020, https://www.washingtonpost.com/opinions/2020/04/14/state-department-cables-warned-safety-issues-wuhan-lab-studying-bat-coronaviruses/.

403. Blumenthal, Max, and Ajit Singh. "How a Trump Media Dump Mainstreamed

Theory That Chinese Lab Manufactured Coronavirus." *The Grayzone*, 20 Apr. 2020, https://thegrayzone.com/2020/04/20/trump-media-chinese-lab-coronavirus-conspiracy/.

404. Andersen, Kristian G., et al. "The Proximal Origin of SARS-COV-2." *Nature*, 17 Mar. 2020, https://www.nature.com/articles/s41591-020-0820-9.

405. "Statement in Support of the Scientists, Public Health Professionals, and Medical Professionals of China Combatting COVID-19." *The Lancet*, 18 Feb. 2020, https://www.thelancet.com/action/showPdf?pii=S0140-6736%2820%2930418-9.

406. The lab leak theory later re-emerged among liberals and Democrats, but journalist Alan MacLeod responded masterfully in a *MintPress* piece entitled, "Unchallenged Orientalism": Why Liberals Suddenly Love the Lab Leak Theory" (https://www.mintpressnews.com/why-liberals-suddenly-love-lab-leak-theory/277882/)

407. "Stop Using Religious Matters to Smear China." *China Daily*, 2 May 2020, https://global.chinadaily.com.cn/a/202005/02/WS5ead443fa310a8b2411533a8.html.

408. Norton, Ben, and Ajit Singh. "No, the UN Did Not Report China Has 'Massive Internment Camps' for Uighur Muslims." *The Grayzone*, 23 Aug. 2018, https://thegrayzone.com/2018/08/23/un-did-not-report-china-internment-camps-uighur-muslims/.

409. See note 408.

410. Sautman, Barry, and Yan Hairong. "Do Supporters of Nobel Winner Liu Xiaobo Really Know What He Stands for? ." *The Guardian*, Guardian News and Media, 15 Dec. 2010, https://www.theguardian.com/commentisfree/2010/dec/15/nobel-winner-liu-xiaobo-chinese-dissident.

411. Chin, Josh. "The German Data Diver Who Exposed China's Muslim Crackdown." *The Wall Street Journal*, Dow Jones & Company, 21 May 2019, https://www.wsj.com/articles/the-german-data-diver-who-exposed-chinas-muslim-crackdown-11558431005.

412. Singh, Ajit, and Max Blumenthal. "China Detaining Millions of Uyghurs? Serious Problems with Claims by US-Backed NGO and Far-Right Researcher 'Led by God' against Beijing." *The Grayzone*, 21 Dec. 2019, https://thegrayzone.com/2019/12/21/china-detaining-millions-uyghurs-problems-claims-us-ngo-researcher/.

413. Smith, Marion. "Blame the Chinese Communist Party for the Coronavirus Crisis." *Victims of Communism*, 5 Apr. 2020, https://victimsofcommunism.org/blame-chinese-communist-party-coronavirus-crisis/.

414. Haiphong, Danny. "My Trip to China Exposed the Shameful Lies Peddled by the American Empire." *Black Agenda Report*, 15 Jan. 2020, https://blackagendareport.com/my-trip-china-exposed-shameful-lies-peddled-american-empire.

415. Askhar, Aybek. "Xinjiang Denies Report about Passports for Uygurs." *China Daily*, 30 Apr. 2020, https://global.chinadaily.com.cn/a/202004/30/WS5eaa171ca310a8b241152c56.html.

416. Singh, Ajit. "'Forced Labor' Stories on China Brought to You by Us Gov, NATO, Arms Industry to Drive Cold War PR Blitz." *The Grayzone*, 26 Mar. 2020, https://thegrayzone.com/2020/03/26/forced-labor-china-us-nato-arms-industry-cold-war/.

417. Westcott, Ben, and Haley Byrd. "US House Passes Uyghur Act Calling for Tough Sanctions on Beijing over Xinjiang Camps." *CNN*, Cable News Network, 4 Dec. 2019, https://www.cnn.com/2019/12/03/politics/us-xinjiang-bill-trump-intl-hnk/index.html.

418. Myerson, Jesse A. "An Anti-China Message Didn't Work for Democrats in 2018 — and It Won't Work for Biden Now." *The Intercept*, 22 Apr. 2020, https://theintercept.com/2020/04/22/biden-china-campaign-ad-trump/.

419. Maté, Aaron. "Don't Let Russophobia Warp the Facts on Russiagate." *The Nation*, 14 Dec. 2018, https://www.thenation.com/article/archive/russiagate-russophobia-mueller-trump/.

420. Tavernise, Sabrina, and Richard A. Oppel. "Spit on, Yelled at, Attacked: Chinese-Americans Fear for Their Safety." *The New York Times*, 23 Mar. 2020, https://www.nytimes.com/2020/03/23/us/chinese-coronavirus-racist-attacks.html.

421. Prashad, Vijay, et al. "China and Coronashock." *Tricontinental*, 28 Apr. 2020, https://thetricontinental.org/studies-2-coronavirus/.

422. Escobar, Pepe. "China Locked in Hybrid War with US." *Asia Times*, 17 Mar. 2020, https://asiatimes.com/2020/03/china-locked-in-hybrid-war-with-us/.

423. "Connecting the Dots: Iran, China, and the Challenge to U.S. Hegemony." Qiao

Collective, 18 Jan. 2020, https://www.qiaocollective.com/articles/iran-china-challenge.

424. "After the West: China's Internationalist Solidarity in the Age of Coronavirus." *Qiao Collective*, 26 Mar. 2020, https://www.qiaocollective.com/articles/internationalist-solidarity-in-the-age-of-coronavirus.

425. "How PR Sold the War in the Persian Gulf." *PR Watch*, 5 June 2013, https://www.prwatch.org/books/tsigfy10.html.

426. Regan, Tom. "When Contemplating War, Beware of Babies in Incubators." *The Christian Science Monitor*, 6 Sept. 2002, https://www.csmonitor.com/2002/0906/p25s02-cogn.html.

427. Taibbi, Matt. "16 Years Later, How the Press That Sold the Iraq War Got Away with It." *Rolling Stone*, 22 Mar. 2019, https://www.rollingstone.com/politics/politics-features/iraq-war-media-fail-matt-taibbi-812230/.

428. Forte, Maximilian. "The Top Ten Myths in the War against Libya." *CounterPunch*, 31 Aug. 2011, https://www.counterpunch.org/2011/08/31/the-top-ten-myths-in-the-war-against-libya/.

429. Maté, Aaron. "Exclusive: New OPCW Whistleblower Slams 'Abhorrent Mistreatment' of Douma Investigators." *The Grayzone*, 12 Mar. 2020, https://thegrayzone.com/2020/03/12/opcw-whistleblower-mistreatment-douma-investigators/.

430. Emersberger, Joe. "Why Venezuela Reporting Is so Bad." *FAIR*, 27 June 2018, https://fair.org/home/why-venezuela-reporting-is-so-bad/.

431. Cohen, Jeff, and Norman Solomon. "30-Year Anniversary: Tonkin Gulf Lie Launched Vietnam War." *FAIR*, 27 July 1994, https://fair.org/media-beat-column/30-year-anniversary-tonkin-gulf-lie-launched-vietnam-war/.

432. "Socialism with Chinese Characteristics-Introductory Study Guide." *Qiao Collective*, 4 Nov. 2021, https://www.qiaocollective.com/education/socialism-with-chinese-characteristics.

433. "How China Lifted 850 Million People out of Extreme Poverty, W/ Tings Chak." *YouTube*, BreakThrough News, 7 Sept. 2021, https://youtu.be/ZuBCr_15BIk.

434. This tweet is no longer available (the user's account was suspended). Previous tweet URL: https://twitter.com/KingOfSorrow420/status/1263984757773406216?s=20.

435. Pollitt, Katha. "We Should Take Women's Accusations Seriously. But Tara Reade's Fall Short." *The Nation*, 20 May 2020, https://www.thenation.com/article/politics/joe-biden-tara-reade-allegations/.

436. "Biden Tells Voters 'You Ain't Black' If You're Still Deciding between Him and Trump – Video." *The Guardian*, Guardian News and Media, 22 May 2020, https://www.theguardian.com/us-news/video/2020/may/22/joe-biden-charlamagne-you-aint-black-trump-video.

437. Breuninger, Kevin. "Joe Biden Tells Factory Worker 'You're Full of s---' during a Tense Argument over Guns." *CNBC*, 11 Mar. 2020, https://www.cnbc.com/2020/03/10/joe-biden-told-an-auto-worker-youre-full-of-shit-during-a-tense-argument-over-guns.html.

438. Greve, Joan E. "'You're a Damn Liar': Biden Lashes out at Voter and Seems to Call Him Fat." *The Guardian*, Guardian News and Media, 5 Dec. 2019, https://www.theguardian.com/us-news/2019/dec/05/joe-biden-iowa-voter-fat.

439. Nagle, Molly [@MollyNagle3]. "'I'm Going to Be Joe Biden,' @JoeBiden Says When Asked If He's Prepared to Govern as a Progressive. 'I Do Not Support Medicare-for-All. I Will Not Support Medicare-for-All ,but I Do Support, Making Sure That Obamacare Is around with a Public Option," He Continues on @CNBC." *Twitter*, 22 May 2020, https://twitter.com/MollyNagle3/status/1263806619261054976?s=20&t=nCOfprQpv3xoEnjZlxybsg.

440. Norton, Benjamin [@BenjaminNorton]. "Once Again, There Are No Significant Political Differences between Donald Trump and Joe Biden. Both Are Right-Wing War Criminals and Racists Who Support Israeli Apartheid and Spit on International Law. Https://T.co/c3zy1alsm1." *Twitter*, 29 Apr. 2020, https://twitter.com/BenjaminNorton/status/1255626360766238720?s=20&t=cPiLbhyD2jFl7V4b0uNzXw.

441. See note 418.

442. Lee, Carol E., et al. "Looking for Obama's Hidden Hand in Candidates Coalescing around Biden." *NBCNews.com*, NBCUniversal News Group, 2 Mar. 2020, https://www.nbcnews.com/politics/2020-election/looking-obama-s-hidden-hand-candidate-coalescing-

around-biden-n1147471.

443. "MSNBC Took Direct Orders from the Clintons & Corporate Democrats." *YouTube*, Secular Talk, 22 May 2020, https://youtu.be/c34jwL3eIlg.

444. "US the Biggest Threat to World Peace in 2013 – Poll." *RT International*, 2 Jan. 2014, https://www.rt.com/news/us-biggest-threat-peace-079/.

445. Day, Meagan. "Decades of Hospital Closures Led to This Disaster." *Jacobin*, 4 Apr. 2020, https://www.jacobinmag.com/2020/04/hospital-closing-shortage-coronavirus.

446. Day, Meagan. "Billionaires Are the Pandemic's Villains, Not Its Heroes." *Jacobin*, 27 Apr. 2020, https://www.jacobinmag.com/2020/04/billionaires-coronvirus-pandemic-profiteers-taxes.

447. Sonnemaker, Tyler. "Jeff Bezos Is on Track to Become a Trillionaire by 2026 - despite an Economy-Killing Pandemic and Losing $38 Billion in His Recent Divorce." *Business Insider*, 14 May 2020, https://www.businessinsider.com/jeff-bezos-on-track-to-become-trillionaire-by-2026-2020-5.

448. Blumenthal, Max. "Iraqi Pm Reveals Soleimani Was on Peace Mission When Assassinated, Exploding Trump's Lie of 'Imminent Attacks.'" *The Grayzone*, 6 Jan. 2020, https://thegrayzone.com/2020/01/06/soleimani-peace-mission-assassinated-trump-lie-imminent-attacks/.

449. "Gen. Soleimani 'Was a War Hero' - Iranian Professor." *YouTube*, The Grayzone, 6 Jan. 2020, https://youtube.com/watch?v=syyv7cu6xbohttps:/youtu.be/ord41k8lgn0.

450. "US Escalates War on Iran and Iraq - Discussion with Rania Khalek, Max Blumenthal, Ben Norton, Aaron Mate." *The Grayzone*, 3 Jan. 2020, https://thegrayzone.com/2020/01/03/us-war-iran-iraq-rania-khalek/.

451. MacLeod, Alan. "Guaidó's Mercenary Hit Contract on Venezuela's Maduro Mirrors Official US Bounty, Authorizes Death Squad Killings." *The Grayzone*, 10 May 2020, https://thegrayzone.com/2020/05/10/guaido-mercenary-contract-venezuelas-maduro-us-bounty-death-squad/.

452. Vaz, Lucas Koerner, and Ricardo Vaz. "Venezuela: Two US Citizens Captured in Botched Coup Attempt." *Venezuelanalysis.com*, 5 May 2020, https://venezuelanalysis.com/news/14864.

453. Maupin, Caleb T. "The Facts about Venezuela's Presidential Election." *MintPress News*, 24 May 2018, https://www.mintpressnews.com/the-facts-about-venezuelas-may-20th-presidential-election/242622/.

454. "Read the Attachments to the General Services Agreement between the Venezuelan Opposition and Silvercorp." *The Washington Post*, WP Company, 6 May 2020, https://www.washingtonpost.com/context/read-the-attachments-to-the-general-services-agreement-between-the-venezuelan-opposition-and-silvercorp/e67f401f-8730-4f66-af53-6a9549b88f94/.

455. Gibbons, Chip. "They're Not Sending Their Best People to Stage a Coup in Venezuela." *Jacobin*, 12 May 2020, https://www.jacobinmag.com/2020/05/coup-venezuela-united-states-maduro-guaido.

456. Koerner, Lucas. "Former US Special Ops Soldier Led Plot to Invade Venezuela: Sources." *Venezuelanalysis.com*, 2 May 2020, https://venezuelanalysis.com/news/14859.

457. See note 454.

458. Vaz, Ricardo, and Lucas Koerner. "US Investigating Ex-Green Beret, Denies 'Direct' Involvement in Failed Venezuela Coup." *Venezuelanalysis.com*, 7 May 2020, https://venezuelanalysis.com/news/14867.

459. Koerner, Lucas, and Ricardo Vaz. "Venezuela: Guaido Embattled as Opposition Splits over New Corruption Scandal." *Venezuelanalysis.com*, 5 Dec. 2019, https://venezuelanalysis.com/news/14739.

460. Cohen, Dan, and Max Blumenthal. "The Making of Juan Guaidó: How the US Regime Change Laboratory Created Venezuela's Coup Leader." *The Grayzone*, 29 Jan. 2019, https://thegrayzone.com/2019/01/29/the-making-of-juan-guaido-how-the-us-regime-change-laboratory-created-venezuelas-coup-leader/.

461. McChesney, Robert W., and Mark Weisbrot. "Venezuela and the Media: FACT and Fiction." *Venezuelanalysis.com*, 2 June 2007, https://venezuelanalysis.com/analysis/2288.

462. Mundial, Yvke. "Plan Conspirativo 'Fiesta Mexicana' Fue Elaborado Hace 10 Años y Costó 52 Mil Dólares, Revela Rodríguez Torres." *Aporrea*, 5 May 2014, https://www.aporrea.

org/actualidad/n250229.html.

463. REDRADIOVE [@RedRadioVe]. "@Jguaido; 'Son Un Mito Los Muertos Por Guayas Del 2014' Según Este Fascista y Responsable En Gran Medida De Los Mas De 43 Muertos En Guarimbas Gracias Al Llamado a La Violencia Del Grupo Vandálico @ Voluntadpopular y Su Lider @Leopoldolopez. No Seas Tan Guaido! PIC.TWITTER. COM/C3TXQNN6AX." *Twitter*, 24 Jan. 2019, https://twitter.com/RedRadioVe/status/1088237230211190790?s=20&t=hUnOF9eawMLJMMygHBLuAw.

464. "Este Es Elvis Durán, El Motorizado Degollado Por La Guaya Tensada Como Barricada (+Fotos)." *Noticas En Tweet*, 22 Feb. 2014, http://notitweet-sucesos.blogspot.com/2014/02/este-es-elvis-duran-el-motorizado.html.

465. "Muere Joven Venezolano Por Guaya Colocada Por Grupos Fascistas." *TeleSUR*, 21 Feb. 2014, https://www.telesurtv.net/news/Muere-joven-venezolano-por-guaya-colocada-por-grupos-fascistas-20140222-0059.html.

466. See note 460.

467. Cook, Mark. "Venezuela Coverage Takes Us Back to Golden Age of Lying about Latin America." *FAIR*, 22 Feb. 2019, https://fair.org/home/venezuela-coverage-takes-us-back-to-golden-age-of-lying-about-latin-america/.

468. See note 284.

469. Parampil, Anya. "The End of Juan Guaidó: Venezuelan Coup Leader Rejected by Country's Opposition." *The Grayzone*, 9 Jan. 2020, https://thegrayzone.com/2020/01/09/the-end-of-juan-guaido-venezuelan-coup-leader-rejected-by-countrys-opposition/.

470. Ward, Alex. "The 'Ridiculous' Failed Coup Attempt in Venezuela, Explained." *Vox*, 11 May 2020, https://www.vox.com/2020/5/11/21249203/venezuela-coup-jordan-goudreau-maduro-guaido-explain.

471. Norton, Ben. "WSJ Confirms: Trump-Appointed Venezuela Coup Leader Plans Neoliberal Capitalist Shock Therapy." *The Grayzone*, 3 Feb. 2019, https://thegrayzone.com/2019/02/03/wsj-venezuela-coup-leader-juan-guaido-neoliberal-capitalist-shock-therapy/.

472. See note 279.

473. Forero, Juan. "Documents Show C.I.A. Knew of a Coup Plot in Venezuela." *The New York Times*, 3 Dec. 2004, https://www.nytimes.com/2004/12/03/washington/world/documents-show-cia-knew-of-a-coup-plot-in-venezuela.html.

474. "China Delivers 71 Tons of Medical Aid to Venezuela." *Venezuelanalysis.com*, 15 May 2019, https://venezuelanalysis.com/news/14490.

475. See note 424.

476. Pompeo, Mike [@SecPompeo]. "As We Mark the 75th Anniversary of the End of the Holocaust, @STATEDEPT'S JUST ACT Report Highlights Countries' Efforts to Provide a Measure of Justice to Holocaust Survivors and Their Families. We Must #Neverforget the Unspeakable Crimes of the Holocaust." *Twitter*, 29 July 2020, https://twitter.com/SecPompeo/status/1288550324056264705?s=20&t=tT67XMBYrwNESWBfCWHOyg.

477. Montoya-Galvez, Camilo. "Thousands of Migrant Children Were Sexually Abused in U.S. Custody, HHS Docs Say." *CBS News*, 27 Feb. 2019, https://www.cbsnews.com/news/thousands-of-migrant-children-were-sexually-abused-in-u-s-custody-hhs-docs-say/.

478. Goodkind, Nicole. "Migrant Detention Center Inspector Tells Congress 'Hellholes' Are Traumatizing Children on Purpose." *Newsweek*, 12 July 2019, https://www.newsweek.com/migrant-detention-center-conditions-child-separation-abuse-trauma-trump-1449043.

479. Breland, Ali. "Nazis Put This Symbol on Political Opponents' Arms. Now Trump Is Using It." *Mother Jones*, 18 June 2020, https://www.motherjones.com/2020-elections/2020/06/trump-upside-down-triangle-antifa/.

480. Matthew John. "American Fascism Invades Portland." *Medium*, Extra Newsfeed, 18 July 2020, https://extranewsfeed.com/american-fascism-invades-portland-1e773e07c2b0.

481. Mahler, Jonathan, and Steve Eder. "'No Vacancies' for Blacks: How Donald Trump Got His Start, and Was First Accused of Bias." *New York Times*, 27 Aug. 2016, https://www.nytimes.com/2016/08/28/us/politics/donald-trump-housing-race.html.

482. Ransom, Jan. "Trump Will Not Apologize for Calling for Death Penalty over Central Park Five." *The New York Times*, 18 June 2019, https://www.nytimes.com/2019/06/18/nyregion/central-park-five-trump.html.

483. Lopez, German. "Trump Is Still Reportedly Pushing His Racist 'Birther' Conspiracy Theory about Obama." *Vox*, 29 Nov. 2017, https://www.vox.com/policy-and-politics/2017/11/29/16713664/trump-obama-birth-certificate.

484. Zeleny, Jeff, et al. "Joe Biden Picks Kamala Harris as His Running Mate." *CNN*, Cable News Network, 11 Aug. 2020, https://www.cnn.com/2020/08/11/politics/biden-vp-pick/index.html.

485. "What Defunding the Police Really Means." *Black Lives Matter*, 6 July 2020, https://blacklivesmatter.com/what-defunding-the-police-really-means/.

486. Summers, Juana. "Kamala Harris Is 1st Woman of Color on a Major Party Presidential Ticket." *NPR*, 11 Aug. 2020, https://www.npr.org/2020/08/11/901479949/kamala-harris-is-1st-woman-of-color-on-a-major-party-presidential-ticket.

487. Hartigan, Rachel. "Kamala Harris Will Be First Woman Vice President. Meet the VP Contenders Who Paved the Way." *National Geographic*, 7 Nov. 2020, https://www.nationalgeographic.com/history/article/at-least-11-women-have-run-for-vice-president.

488. Bazelon, Lara. "Kamala Harris Was Not a 'Progressive Prosecutor.'" *New York Times*, 17 Jan. 2019, https://www.nytimes.com/2019/01/17/opinion/kamala-harris-criminal-justice.html.

489. "As San Francisco DA, Kamala Harris's Office Stopped Cooperating With Victims of Clergy Abuse." *YouTube*, The Intercept, 9 June 2019, https://youtu.be/7sVswKxx9dw.

490. Johnson, Chris. "Harris Seeks to Block Gender Reassignment for Trans Inmate." *Washington Blade*, 5 May 2015, https://www.washingtonblade.com/2015/05/05/harris-renews-effort-to-block-gender-reassignment-for-trans-inmate/.

491. Gray, Briahna. "A Problem for Kamala Harris: Can a Prosecutor Become President in the Age of Black Lives Matter?" *The Intercept*, 20 Jan. 2019, https://theintercept.com/2019/01/20/a-problem-for-kamala-harris-can-a-prosecutor-become-president-in-the-age-of-black-lives-matter/.

492. Strangio, Chase. "I'm Not Ready to Trust Kamala Harris on LGBTQ+ Issues." *Out Magazine*, 5 Feb. 2019, https://www.out.com/news-opinion/2019/2/04/kamala-harris-lgbtq-trans-prison.

493. "Biden's Description of Obama Draws Scrutiny." *CNN*, Cable News Network, 9 Feb. 2007, https://www.cnn.com/2007/POLITICS/01/31/biden.obama/.

494. Matthew John. "Is #MeToo Finally Catching up with Joe Biden?" *Medium*, Dialogue & Discourse, 25 Mar. 2020, https://medium.com/discourse/is-metoo-finally-catching-up-with-joe-biden-1354b640870.

495. Greenhouse, Linda. "Ruth Bader Ginsburg, Supreme Court's Feminist Icon, Is Dead at 87." *The New York Times*, 18 Sept. 2020, https://www.nytimes.com/2020/09/18/us/ruth-bader-ginsburg-dead.html.

496. Lerer, Lisa. "R.I.P., R.B.G. What's next?" *The New York Times*, 21 Sept. 2020, https://www.nytimes.com/2020/09/21/us/politics/rbg-election-scotus-trump.html.

497. Goldmacher, Shane, and Jeremy W. Peters. "How Ginsburg's Death Has Reshaped the Money Race for Senate Democrats." *The New York Times*, 21 Sept. 2020, https://www.nytimes.com/2020/09/21/us/politics/ginsburg-senate-donations.html.

498. Baker, Peter, and Nicholas Fandos. "Republican Senators Line up to Back Trump on Court Fight." *The New York Times*, 22 Sept. 2020, https://www.nytimes.com/2020/09/21/us/politics/trump-supreme-court.html.

499. Karni, Annie. "Ginsburg Will Lie in State in the Capitol, the First Woman to Be given the Honor." *The New York Times*, 21 Sept. 2020, https://www.nytimes.com/2020/09/21/us/politics/ginsburg-lie-in-state.html.

500. Crouse, Lindsay. "I Was Tired of Training. but Then I Thought of R.B.G." *The New York Times*, 22 Sept. 2020, https://www.nytimes.com/2020/09/22/opinion/rbg-ginsburg-fitness.html.

501. Blumenthal, Max. "The Other Side of John McCain." *Consortium News*, 27 Aug. 2018, https://consortiumnews.com/2018/08/27/the-other-side-of-john-mccain/.

502. Vogue, Ariane de. "Ruth Bader Ginsburg on Kaepernick Protests: 'I Think It's Dumb and Disrespectful.'" *CNN*, Cable News Network, 12 Oct. 2016, https://www.cnn.com/2016/10/10/politics/ruth-bader-ginsburg-colin-kaepernick/index.html.

503. Haltiwanger, John. "Ruth Bader Ginsburg Defends Brett Kavanaugh, Says He's a

'Very Decent' Man." *Business Insider*, 25 July 2019, https://www.businessinsider.com/ruth-bader-ginsburg-says-brett-kavanaugh-very-decent-man-2019-7.

504. Lind, Dara. "Read Justice Ginsburg's Moving Tribute to Her 'Best Buddy' Justice Scalia." *Vox*, 14 Feb. 2016, https://www.vox.com/2016/2/14/10990156/scalia-ginsburg-friends.

505. Totenberg, Nina. "Supreme Court Sides with Trump Administration in Asylum Cases." *NPR*, 25 June 2020, https://www.npr.org/2020/06/25/883312496/supreme-court-sides-with-trump-administration-in-deportation-case.

506. Kinder, David. "The Rise of the Ruth Bader Ginsburg Cult ." *Current Affairs*, 10 Mar. 2016, https://www.currentaffairs.org/2016/03/the-rise-of-the-ruth-bader-ginsburg-cult.

507. Oberg, Michael Leroy. "On the Notorious RBG and Sherrill." *Native America: A History*, 29 Mar. 2017, https://michaelleroyoberg.com/uncategorized/on-the-notorious-rbg-and-sherrill/.

508. Newcomb, Steve. "Five Hundred Years of Injustice: The Legacy of Fifteenth Century Religious Prejudice." *Indigenous Law Institute*, http://ili.nativeweb.org/sdrm_art.html.

509. "Salazar v. Ramah Navajo Chapter." *Legal Information Institute*, Cornell Law School, https://www.law.cornell.edu/supremecourt/text/11-551.

510. "Kiowa Tribe of OK V. Manufacturing Technologies, Inc., 523 U.S. 751 (1998)." *Legal Information Institute*, Cornell Law School, https://www.law.cornell.edu/supct/html/96-1037.ZS.html.

511. "Inyo County v. Paiute-Shoshone Indians Ofbishop Community of Bishop Colony." *Legal Information Institute*, Cornell Law School, https://www.law.cornell.edu/supremecourt/text/02-281.

512. "Alaska v. Native Village of Venetie Tribal Government, 522 U.S. 520 (1998)." *Legal Information Institute*, Cornell Law School, https://www.law.cornell.edu/supct/html/96-1577.ZS.html.

513. "C & L Enterprises, Inc.. v. Citizen Bandpotawatomi Tribe of OKLA.SYLLABUS." *Legal Information Institute*, Cornel Law School, https://www.law.cornell.edu/supct/html/00-292.ZS.html.

514. "Navajo Nation v. United States Forest Serv. - Opposition." *The United States Department of Justice*, https://www.justice.gov/osg/brief/navajo-nation-v-united-states-forest-serv-opposition.

515. Liptak, Adam. "Supreme Court Rules against Worker Pay for Screenings in Amazon Warehouse Case." *The New York Times*, 9 Dec. 2014, https://www.nytimes.com/2014/12/10/business/supreme-court-rules-against-worker-pay-for-security-screenings.html?_r=0.

516. Stern, Mark Joseph. "Sonia Sotomayor Issues a Stunning Dissent against Police Brutality." *Slate Magazine*, 9 Nov. 2015, https://slate.com/news-and-politics/2015/11/sonia-sotomayor-dissents-in-mullenix-police-shooting-case.html.

517. "Scott v. Harris." *Legal Information Institute*, Cornell Law School, https://www.law.cornell.edu/supremecourt/text/05-1631.

518. Robinson, Nathan J. "The Clintons Had Slaves ." *Current Affairs*, 6 June 2017, https://www.currentaffairs.org/2017/06/the-clintons-had-slaves.

519. MacGuill, Dan. "Fact Check: Did Abraham Lincoln Express Opposition to Racial Equality?" *Snopes*, 16 Aug. 2017, https://www.snopes.com/fact-check/did-lincoln-racism-equality-oppose/.

520. Gordon, Aaron. "Abraham Lincoln Wanted the Freed Slaves to Leave America." *Pacific Standard*, 23 Apr. 2013, https://psmag.com/news/remember-that-time-abraham-lincoln-tried-to-get-the-slaves-to-leave-america-55802.

521. Wiener, Jon. "Largest Mass Execution in US History: 150 Years Ago Today." *The Nation*, 26 Dec. 2012, https://www.thenation.com/article/archive/largest-mass-execution-us-history-150-years-ago-today/.

522. Ritchie, Hannah, and Max Roser. "Gender Ratio." *Our World in Data*, 13 June 2019, https://ourworldindata.org/gender-ratio.

523. Gimenez, Martha E. "Women, Class, and Identity Politics." *Monthly Review*, 1 Sept. 2019, https://monthlyreview.org/2019/09/01/women-class-and-identity-politics/.

524. Hunter, Rob. "The Supreme Court after Scalia." *Jacobin*, 15 Feb. 2016, https://www.jacobinmag.com/2016/02/supreme-court-antonin-scalia-death-nomination-bernie-sanders.

525. Robinson, Nathan J. "The Clintons Had Slaves." *Current Affairs*, 6 June 2017, https://

www.currentaffairs.org/2017/06/the-clintons-had-slaves.

526. Mutabaruka, Moses. "The Emancipation of Women... Speech by Thomas Sankara." *TAP Magazine*, 13 June 2015, https://www.tapmagonline.com/tap/the-emancipation-of-women-speech-by-thomas-sankara.

527. Kasky, Jeffrey. "Poll Workers Signed up to Help Voters. Instead, We Were Abused by Trump Supporters: Opinion." *Sun-Sentinel*, 4 Nov. 2020, https://www.sun-sentinel.com/opinion/commentary/fl-op-com-polling-sites-campaign-intimidation-20201104-rfr6d6npune7daoihytqsogbhq-story.html.

528. Speri, Alice. "The FBI Has Quietly Investigated White Supremacist Infiltration of Law Enforcement." *The Intercept*, 31 Jan. 2017, https://theintercept.com/2017/01/31/the-fbi-has-quietly-investigated-white-supremacist-infiltration-of-law-enforcement/.

529. Matthew John. "American Fascism Invades Portland." *Medium*, Extra Newsfeed, 20 July 2020, https://extranewsfeed.com/american-fascism-invades-portland-1e773e07c2b0.

530. Matthew John. "We Need to Talk about Systemic Racism." *Medium*, An Injustice!, 5 June 2020, https://aninjusticemag.com/we-need-to-talk-about-systemic-racism-50041e835d3d.

531. Carter, Lee [@carterforva] "Joe Biden just issued a statement calling for the arrest of anarchists, simply for BEING anarchists, which is very explicitly not illegal. It should also be noted that Biden and Trump have now joined together in openly calling for the political persecution of the same people." *Twitter*, 28 July 2020, https://twitter.com/carterforva/status/1288221642968236032.

532. "Read the Full Transcript of Joe Biden's ABC News Town Hall." *ABC News*, 15 Oct. 2020, https://abcnews.go.com/Politics/read-full-transcript-joe-bidens-abc-news-town/story?id=73643517.

533. "Flashback: In 1992, Biden Said His Crime Bill Would Do Everything but Hang People for Jaywalking." *YouTube*, GOP War Room, 20 June 2019, https://youtu.be/fVgNB1rr6Mg.

534. Brehm, Sheila. "Michigan's 'Poisoner-in-Chief' Endorses Biden for President." *World Socialist Web Site*, 4 Sept. 2020, https://www.wsws.org/en/articles/2020/09/04/snyd-s04.html.

535.

536. Leber, Rebecca. "No, Biden Won't Ban Fracking." *Mother Jones*, 22 Oct. 2020, https://www.motherjones.com/environment/2020/10/no-biden-wont-ban-fracking/.

537. Daugherty, Owen. "Biden Says He Won't Legalize Marijuana Because It May Be a 'Gateway Drug'." *TheHill*, 17 Nov. 2019, https://thehill.com/homenews/campaign/470861-biden-says-he-wont-legalize-marijuana-because-it-may-be-a-gateway-drug.

538. Cassella, Megan, and Alice Miranda Ollstein. "Biden Eyes GOP Candidates for Cabinet Slots." *POLITICO*, 20 Oct. 2020, https://www.politico.com/news/2020/10/20/biden-transition-republican-cabinet-429972.

539. "How the Electoral College Breaks Democracy." *YouTube*, The Gravel Institute, 2 Nov. 2020, https://youtu.be/-lk1kVd0eW0.

540. Lazare, Daniel. "Abolish the Senate." *Jacobin*, 2 Dec. 2014, https://www.jacobinmag.com/2014/12/abolish-the-senate/.

541. Hayes, Mike, et al. "Derek Chauvin Guilty in Death of George Floyd." *CNN*, Cable News Network, 21 Apr. 2021, https://www.cnn.com/us/live-news/derek-chauvin-trial-04-20-21/index.html.

542. Vera, Amir, et al. "Ohio Officials Release More Body Cam Video of Fatal Police Shooting of Black Teen and Urge Community to Await the Facts." *CNN*, Cable News Network, 22 Apr. 2021, https://www.cnn.com/2021/04/21/us/ohio-columbus-police-shooting-15-year-old/index.html.

543. Truesdell, Jeff. "Since Start of Derek Chauvin Trial, U.S. Police Have Killed an Average of 3 People per Day: Report." *People*, 19 Apr. 2021, https://people.com/crime/police-killed-64-people-since-start-derek-chauvin-trial/.

544. Halper, Evan, et al. "'George's Legacy': Guilty Verdict in Floyd's Murder Reenergizes Democrats' Push for Reform." *Los Angeles Times*, 20 Apr. 2021, https://www.latimes.com/politics/story/2021-04-20/chauvin-floyd-verdict-reaction.

545. Andrew, Scottie, et al. "Biden Opposes Defunding the Police. Here's What That Means." *CNN*, Cable News Network, 14 Apr. 2021, https://www.cnn.com/2021/02/17/politics/

defunding-police-biden-town-hall-trnd/index.html.

546. Moe, Alex [@alexmoeflo]. ".@SpeakerPelosi Speaking at Presser with CBC: Thank You George Floyd for Sacrificing Your Life for Justice...because of You and Because of Thousands, Millions of People around the World Who Came out for Justice, Your Name Will Always Be Synonymous for Justice." *Twitter*, 20 Apr. 2021, https://twitter.com/alexmoeflo/status/1384619869119918083?s=20&t=3fp-OWMPtlSn6K5wF4nM4Q.

547. Ross, Janell. "Police Officers Convicted for Fatal Shootings Are the Exception, Not the Rule." *NBC News*, NBCUniversal News Group, 14 Mar. 2019, https://www.nbcnews.com/news/nbcblk/police-officers-convicted-fatal-shootings-are-exception-not-rule-n982741.

548. "George Floyd's Family Reacts to the Verdict." *YouTube*, Los Angeles Times, 20 Apr. 2021, https://www.youtube.com/watch?v=c_nlvdCIgZM.

549. Olding, Rachel. "George Floyd Protests Likely to Be Largest Movement in U.S. History." *The Daily Beast*, The Daily Beast Company, 3 July 2020, https://www.thedailybeast.com/george-floyd-protests-likely-to-be-largest-movement-in-us-history.

550. Lenin, V.I. "Certain Features of the Historical Development of Marxism." *Marxists Internet Archive*, 28 Dec. 1910, https://www.marxists.org/archive/lenin/works/1910/dec/23.htm.

551. Lenin, V.I. "The Three Sources and Three Component Parts of Marxism." *Marxists Internet Archive*, Mar. 1913, https://www.marxists.org/archive/lenin/works/1913/mar/x01.htm.

552. Parenti, Michael. *Blackshirts and Reds*. City Lights Books, 1997.

553. Guillory, Sean. "Why Should Bernie Sanders Apologize for Communism?" *The Moscow Times*, 3 Mar. 2020, https://www.themoscowtimes.com/2020/03/03/why-should-bernie-sanders-apologize-for-communism-a69509.

554. The elephant in the room is "The Squad." While I want to steer clear of ad hominem attacks, I feel as though I should briefly clarify my current position on the matter (especially since I previously indicated optimism regarding this development). I'll start by reiterating the same general sentiments I expressed regarding both Bernie Sanders and Barack Obama; without speculating about the motives, intentions, or actual ideologies of those in question, the hitherto record of The Squad represents another "best-case scenario" of working within the confines of a bourgeois political system. That being said, the public statements and congressional votes of members of The Squad are a matter of public record. The fact is that AOC and other "progressives" in Congress have increasingly gone along with the Democratic Party's agenda (which, as I have stated, is inherently imperialist and bourgeois). They are, after all, members of said party. The Squad (and the effort at a "progressive insurgency" within the Democratic Party more broadly) is not an effort of communists or revolutionaries, but of reformers. An analysis could be made of (for instance) all of AOC's votes and statements of support for the likes of Joe Biden, Nancy Pelosi, U.S.-aligned movements (including reactionary ones) around the world, etc. (and whether or not this is some elaborate game of 4-D chess aimed at incremental change), but I just feel as though this analysis is both outside the scope of this book and ultimately redundant, based on the statements and clarifications I have already made. Suffice it to say that the Democratic Party has proven it is not and cannot be a vehicle for large-scale progressive change in the United States.

555. Rojas, Rachael Boothroyd. "Collectives Hijack Polar Company Trucks in Caracas, Protest Hoarding." *Venezuelanalysis.com*, 19 Feb. 2016, https://venezuelanalysis.com/news/11861.

556. "Venezuela Protesters Set 40 Tons of Subsidized Food on Fire." *TeleSUR English*, TeleSUR, 30 June 2017, https://www.telesurenglish.net/news/Venezuela-Protesters-Set-40-Tons-of-Subsidized-Food-on-Fire-20170630-0017.html.

557. Debs, Eugene V. "'This Is Our Year ' - But Two Parties And But One Issue." 16 June 1912, Chicago, Riverside Park. https://www.marxists.org/archive/debs/works/1912/twoparties.htm.

558. Cruz, Carlos. "Scandinavia's Covert Role in Western Imperialism." *TeleSUR English*, TeleSUR, 20 Mar. 2017, https://www.telesurenglish.net/analysis/Scandinavias-Covert-Role-in-Western-Imperialism-20170320-0022.html. Accessed 31 Jan. 2022.

559. Marx, Karl. "Critique of the Gotha Programme." *Marxists.org*, https://www.marxists.org/archive/marx/works/1875/gotha/ch04.htm.

Made in United States
Troutdale, OR
01/02/2024